INNOVATIVE MANDALA PATTERN

The Ultimate Mandala Design Pattern For Adults For Stress

Mandala Craft Art

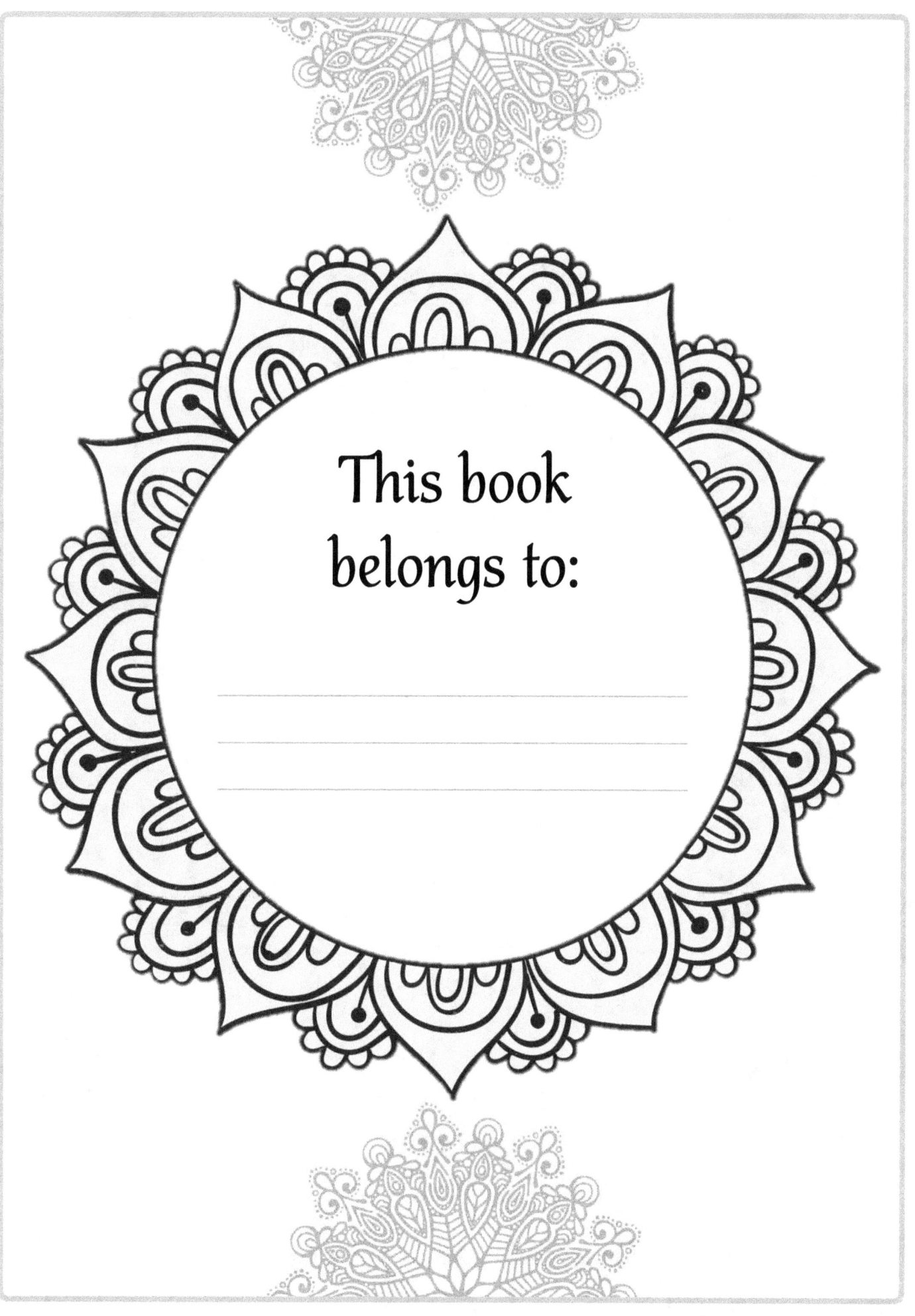

This book
belongs to:

_____

_____

_____

Color Swatch

Test your color supplies on this page to see how they react to the paper. Place a blank page or two behind each page as your color, to prevent bleed-through to the next page.

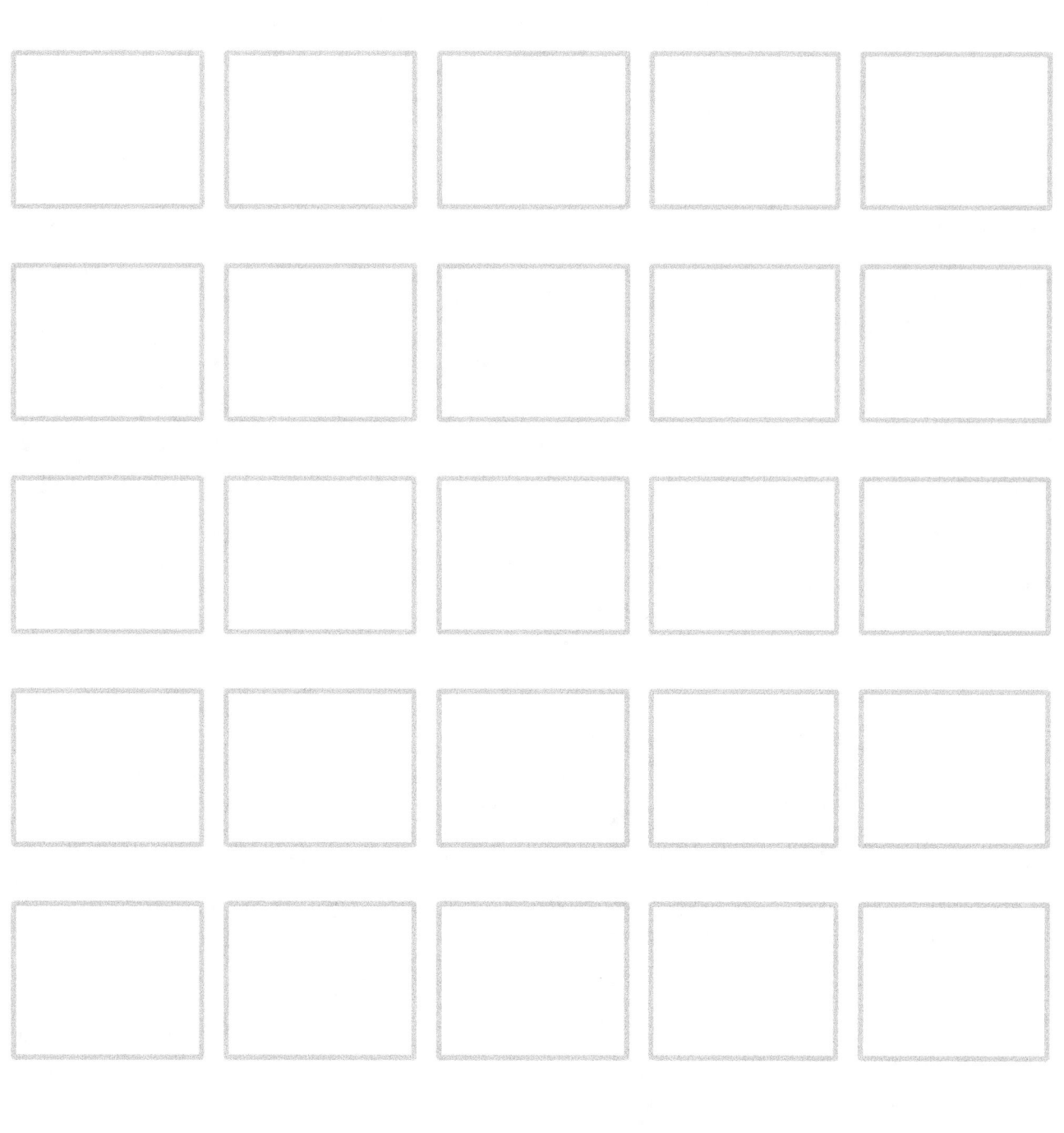

Color this mandala!

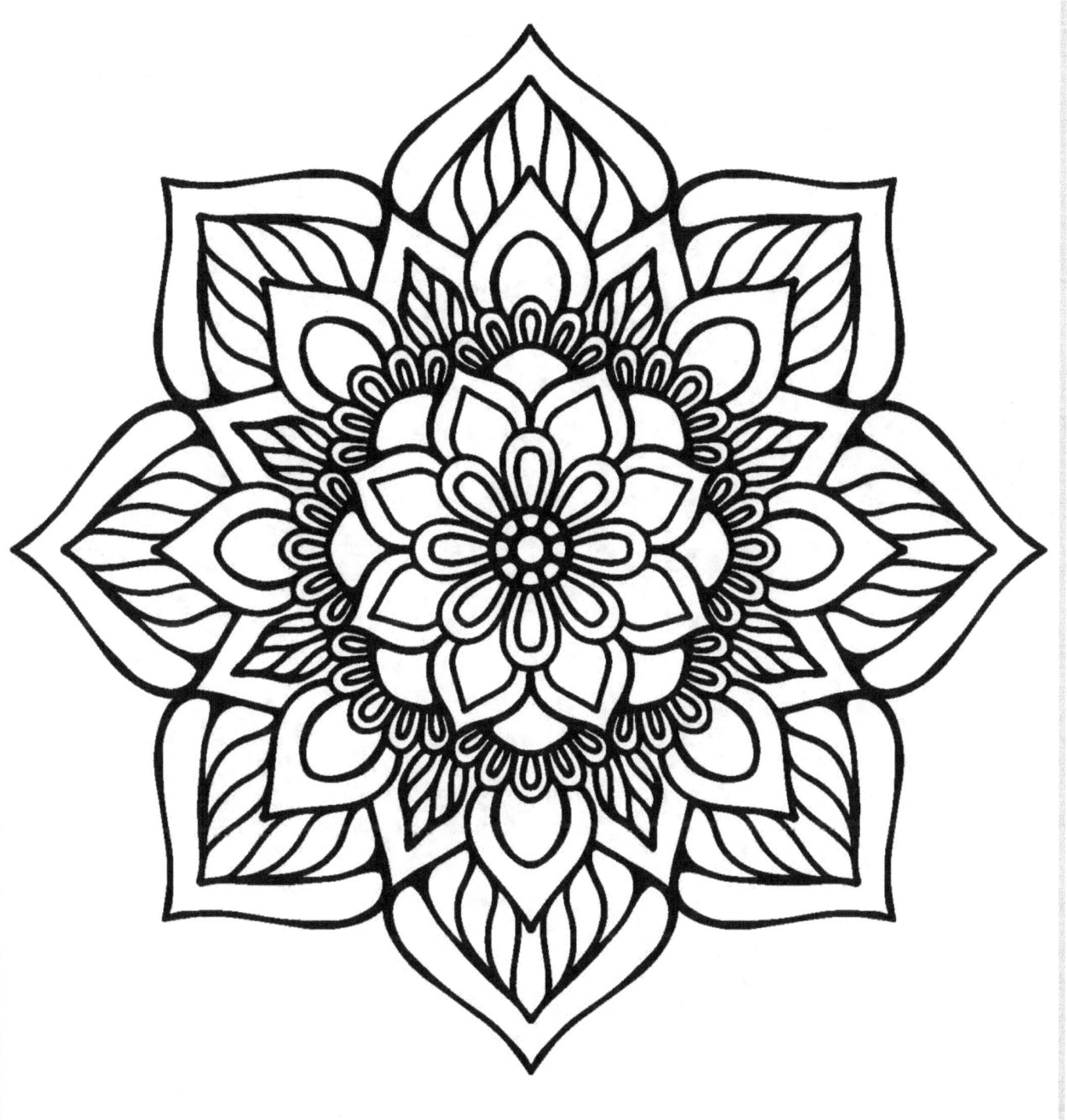

Color this mandala!

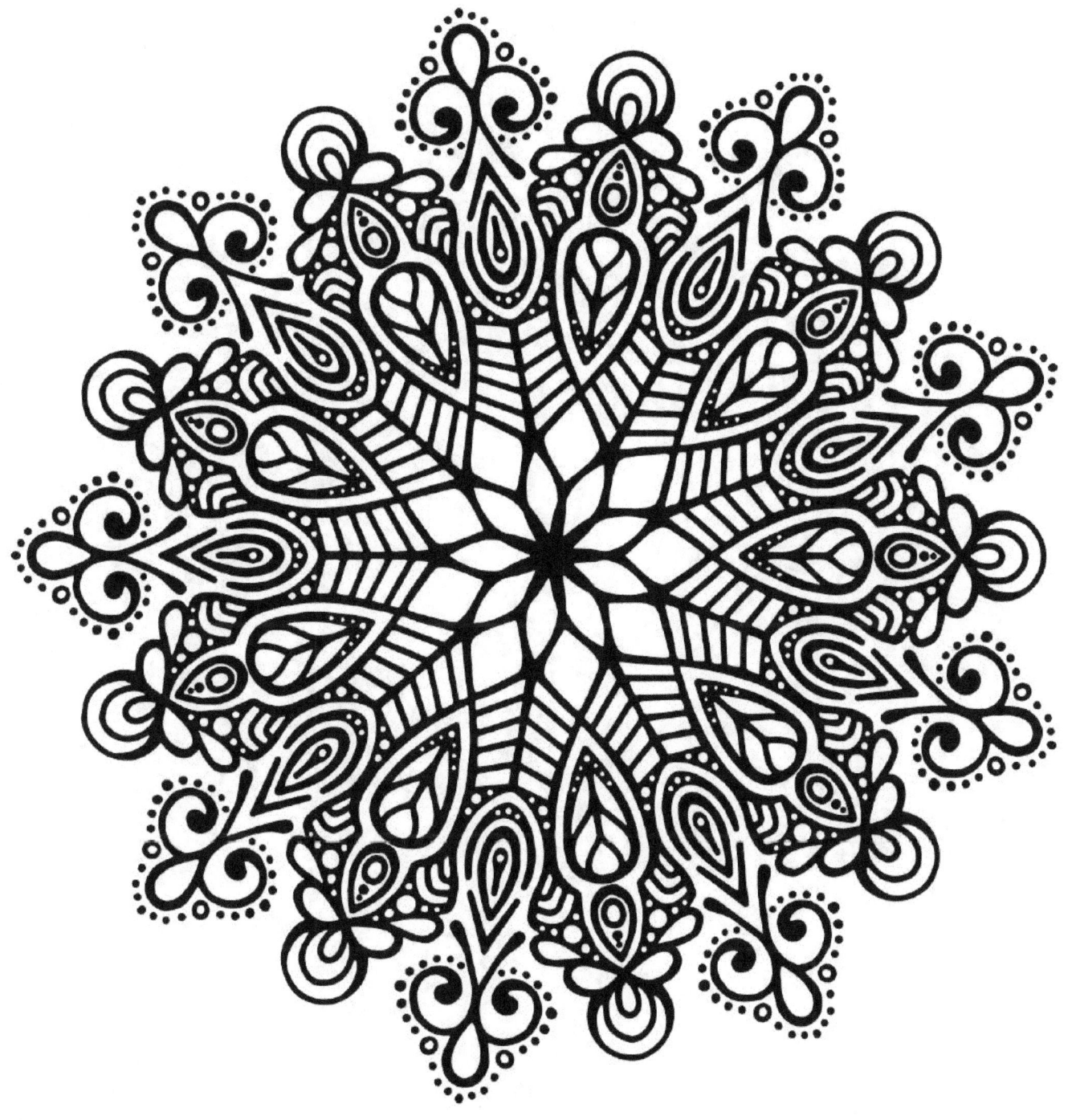

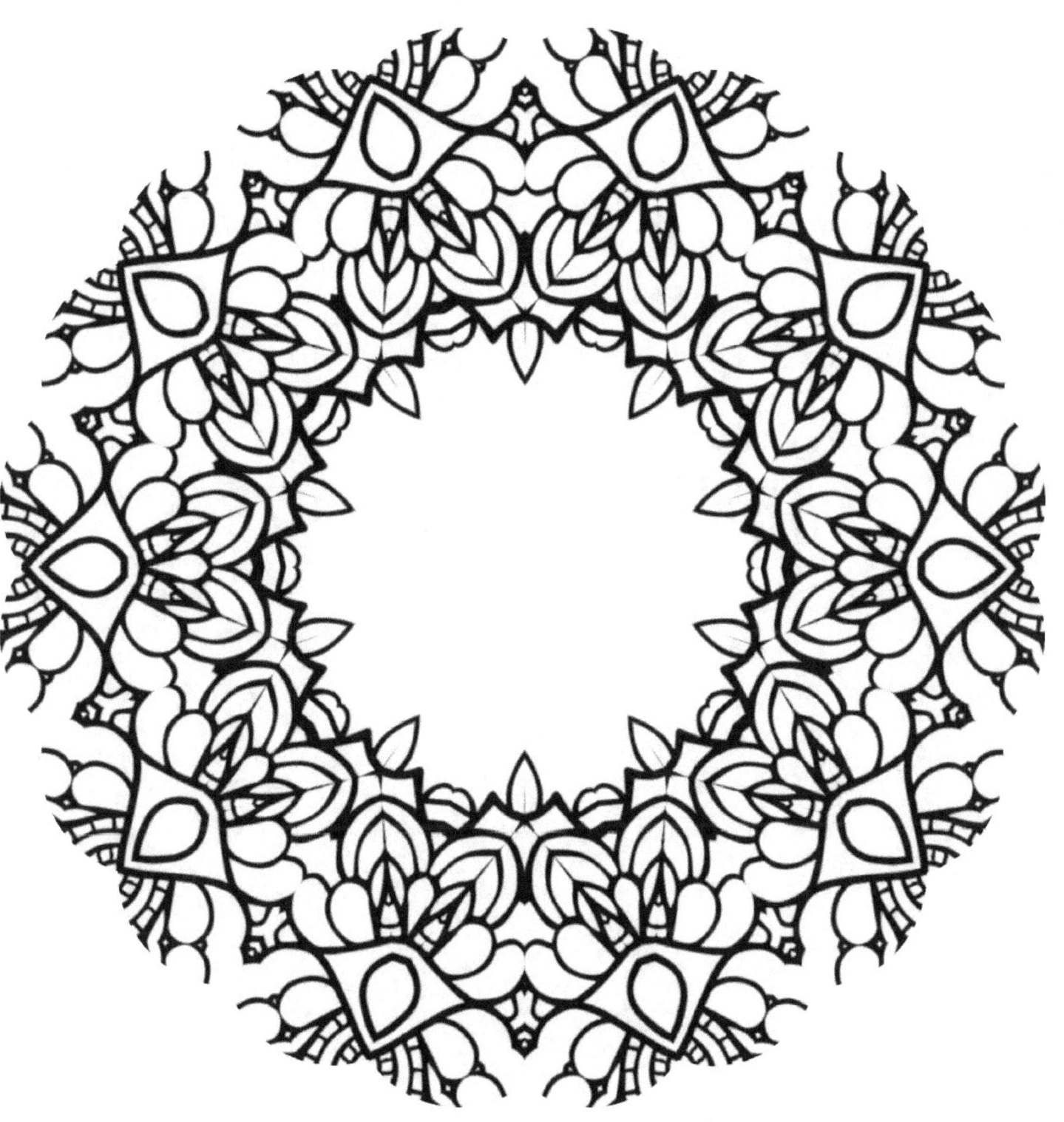

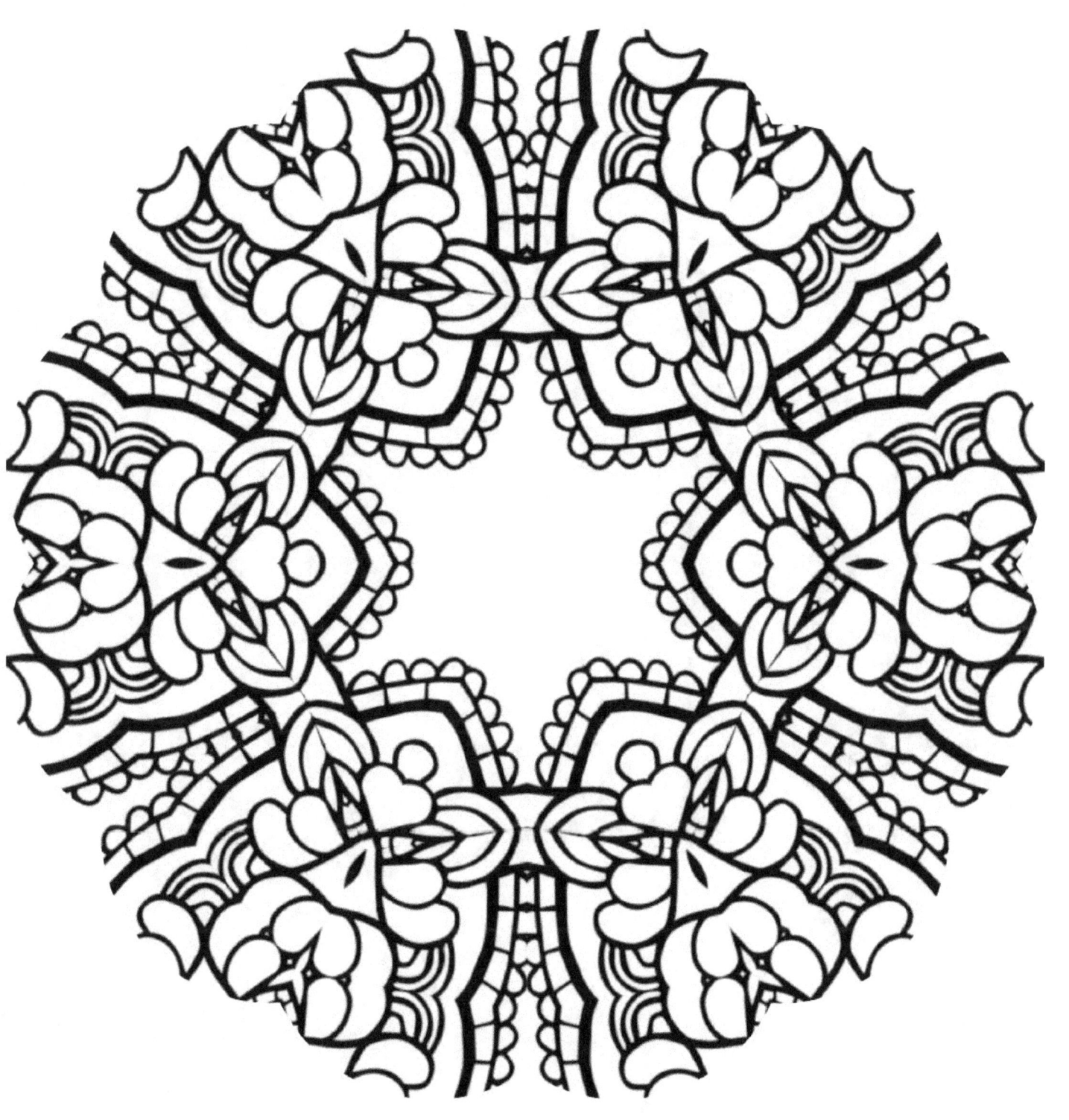

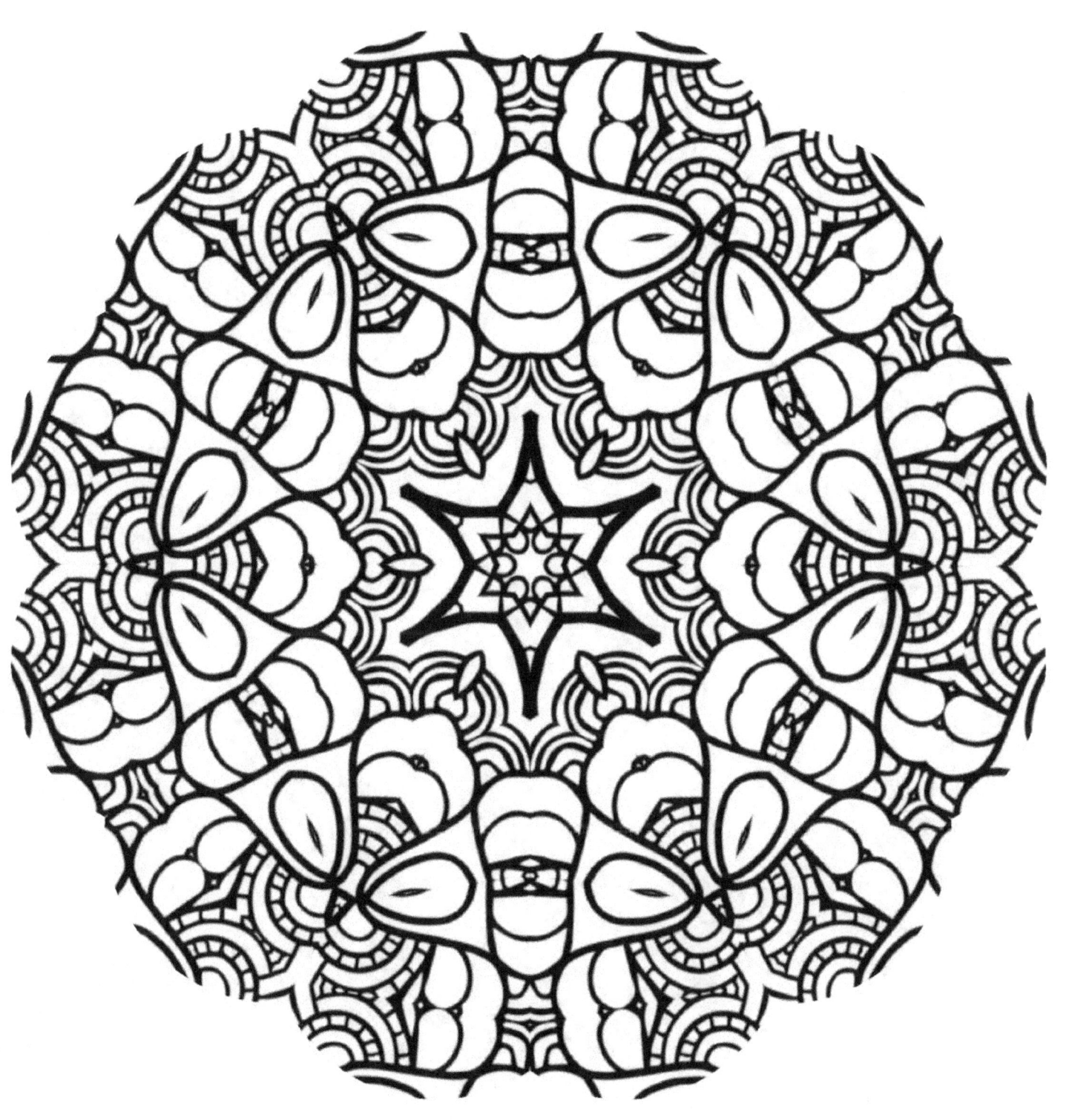

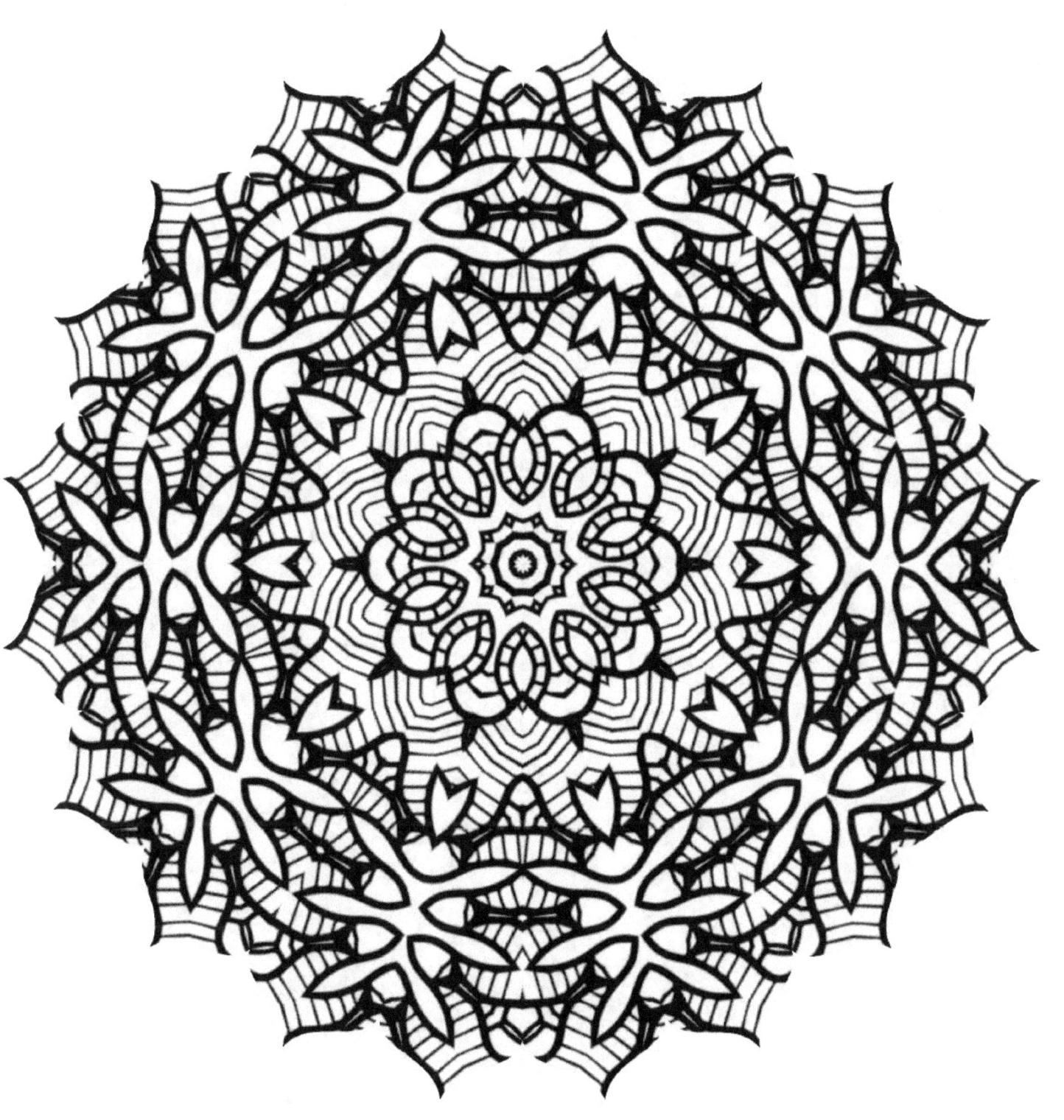

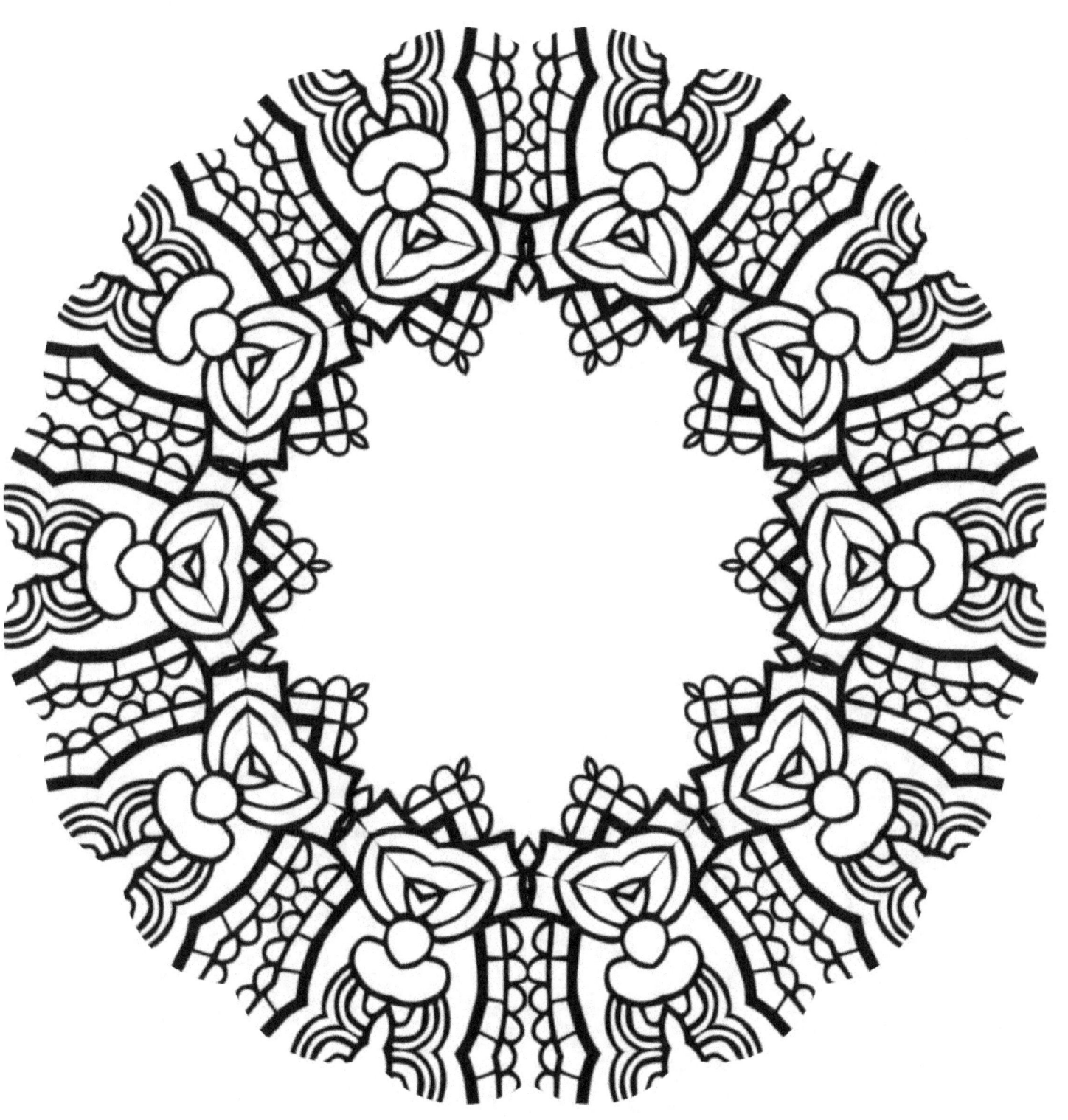

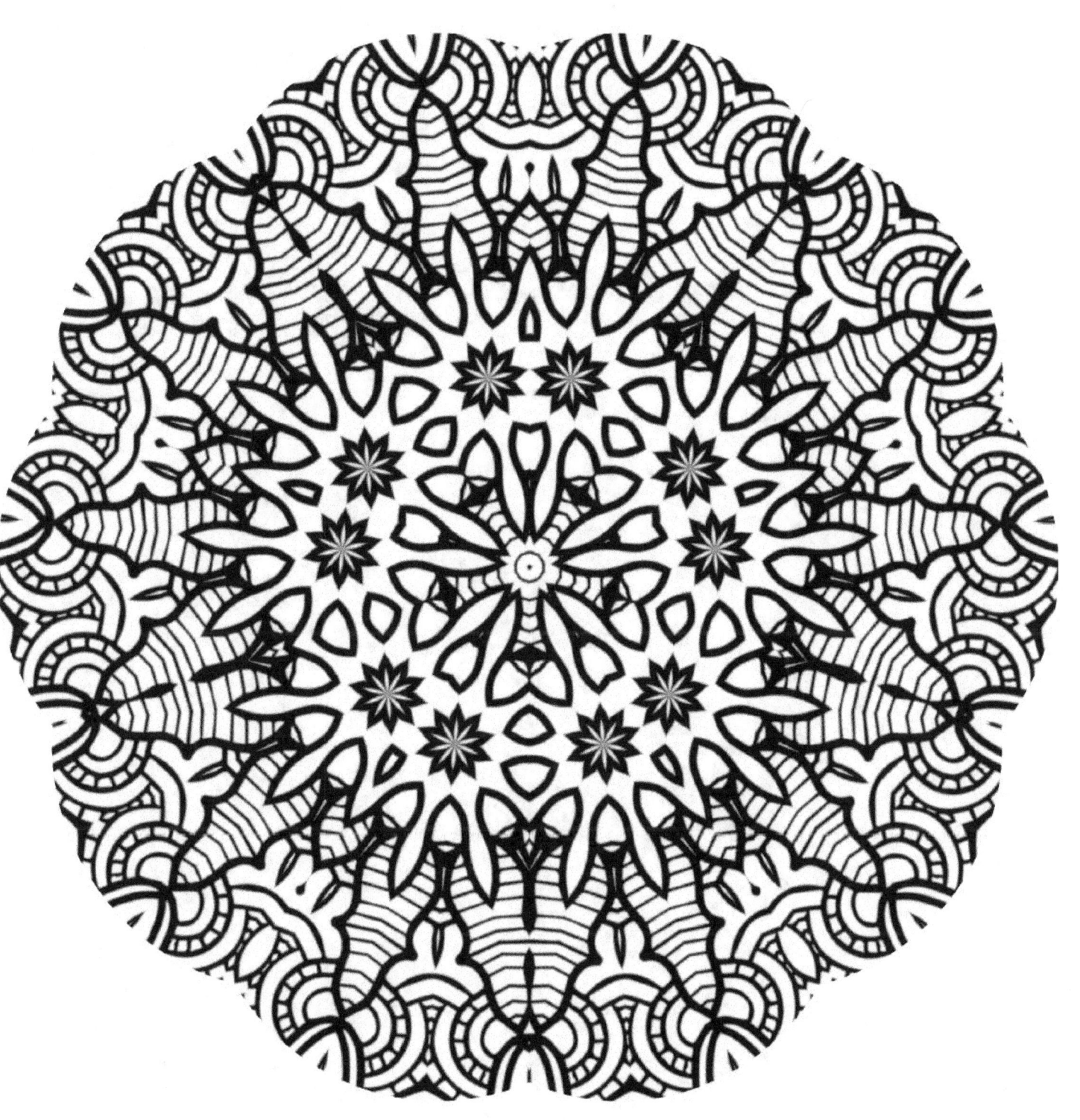

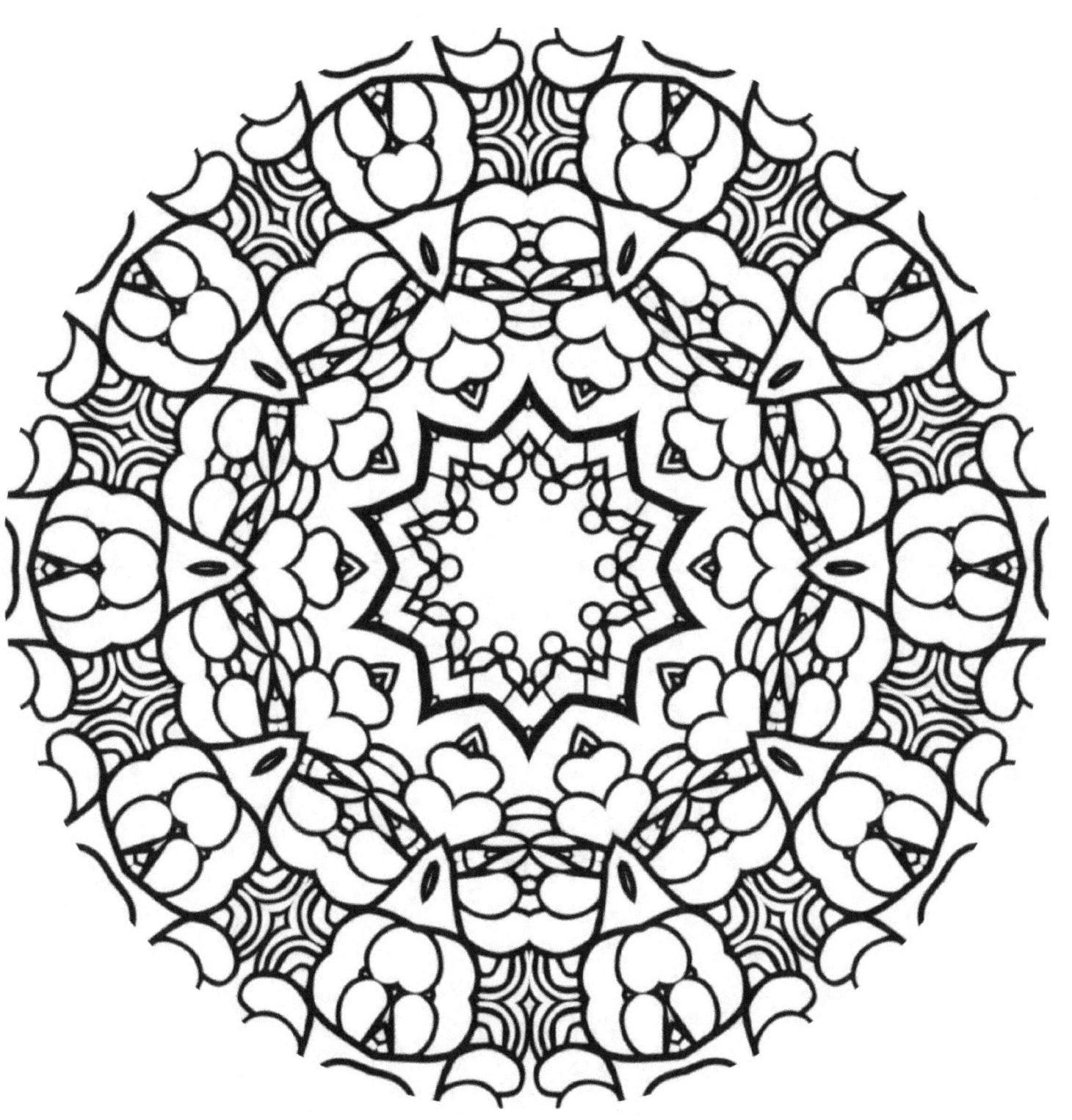

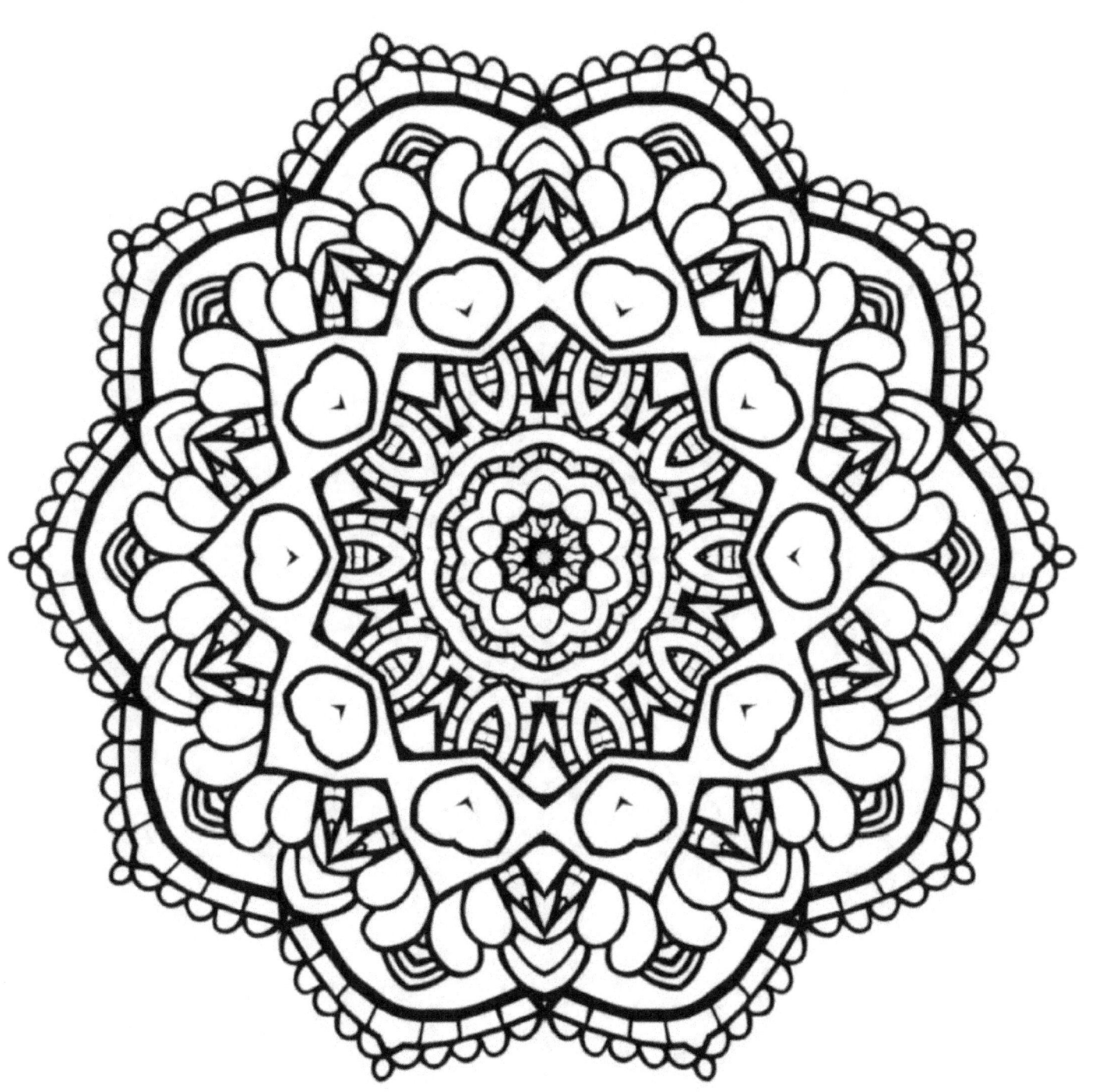

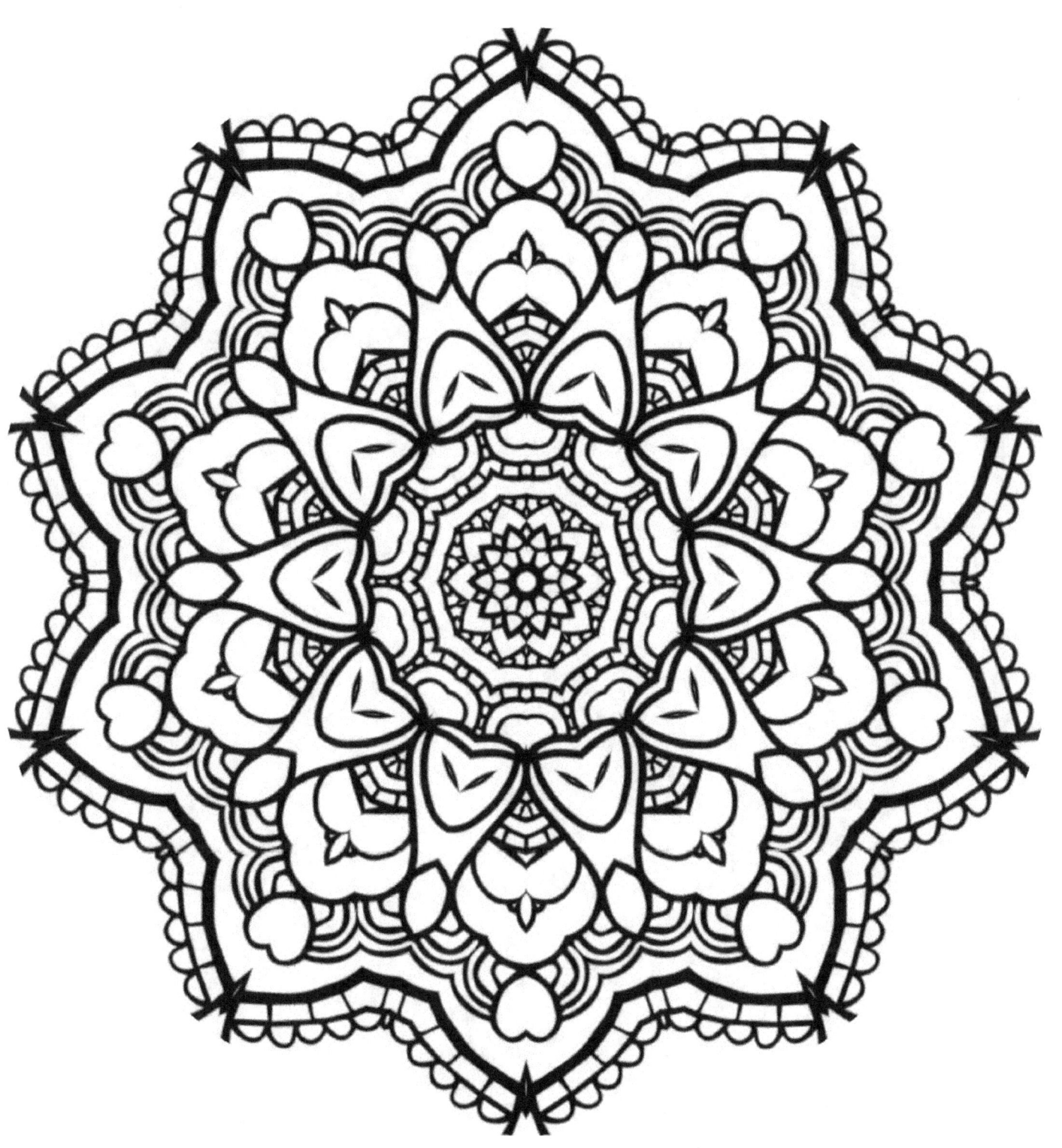

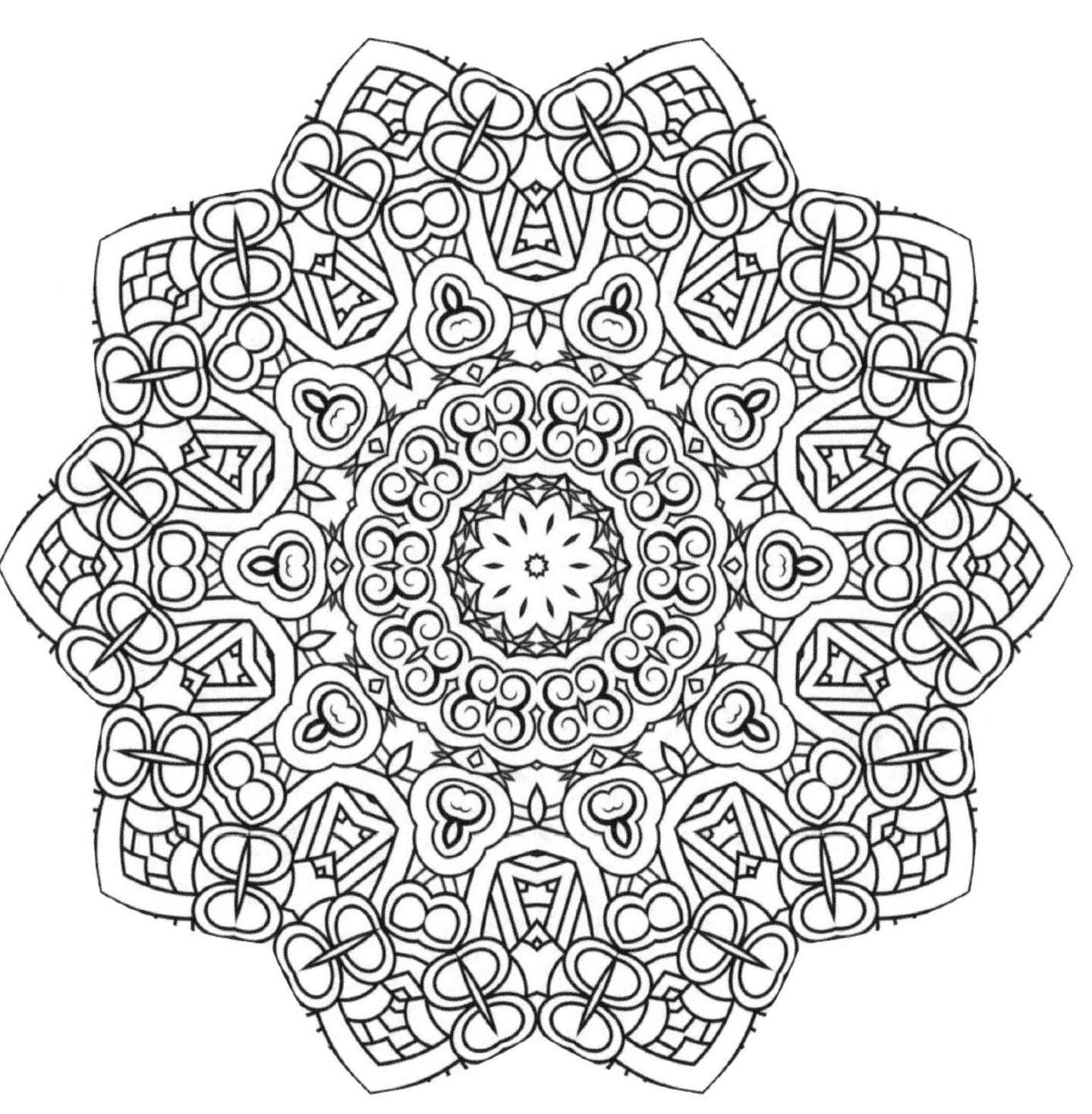

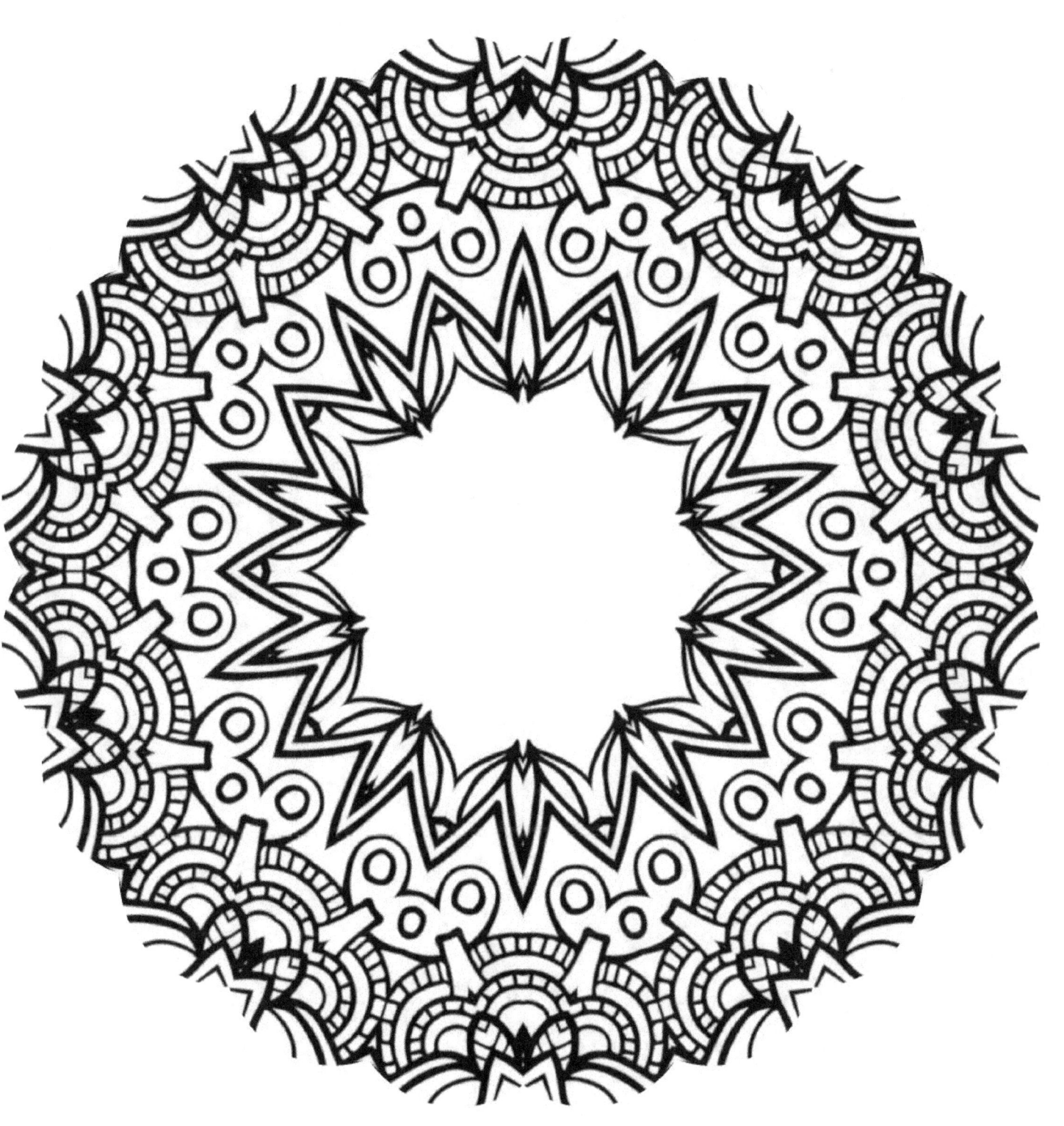

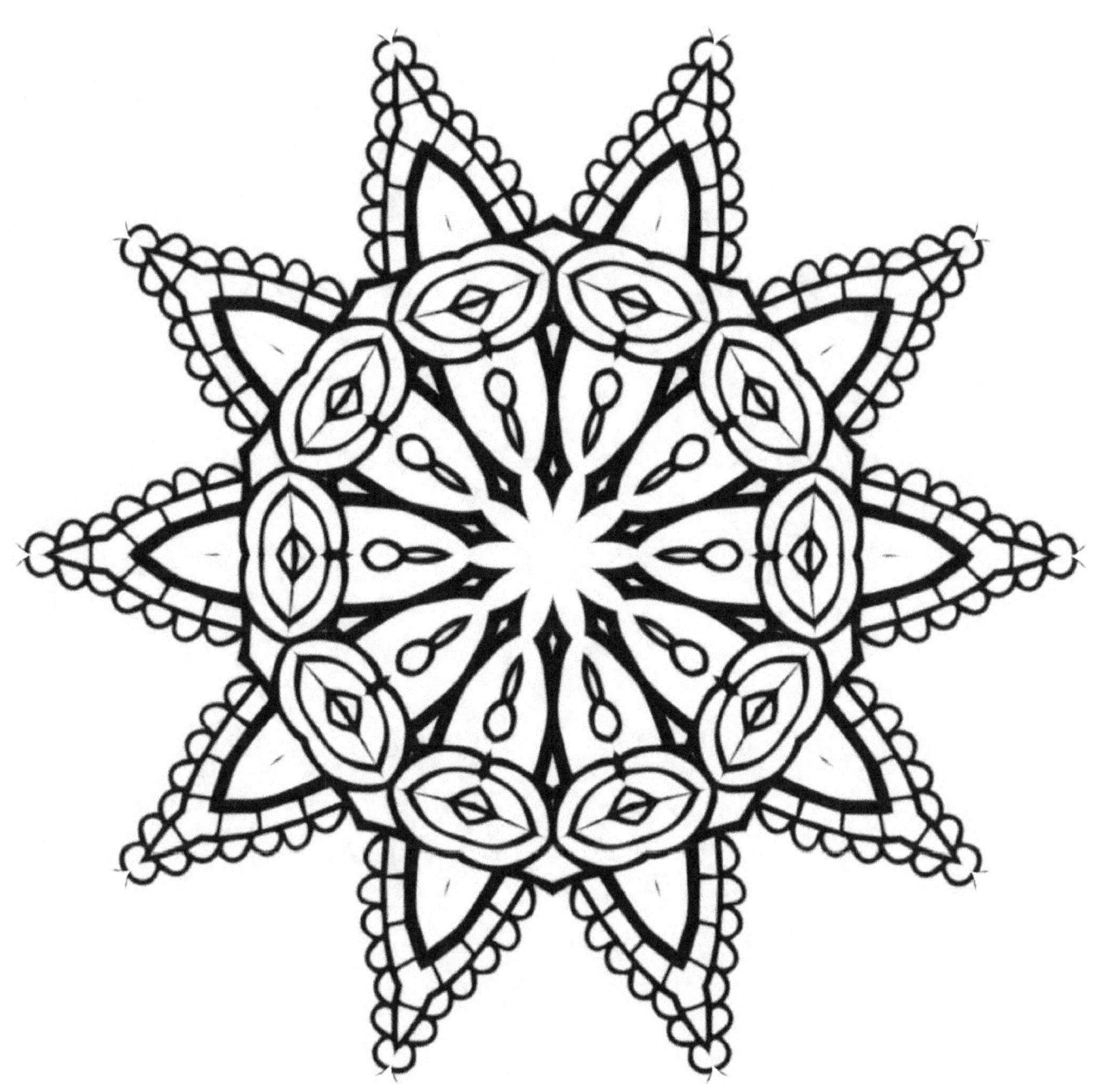

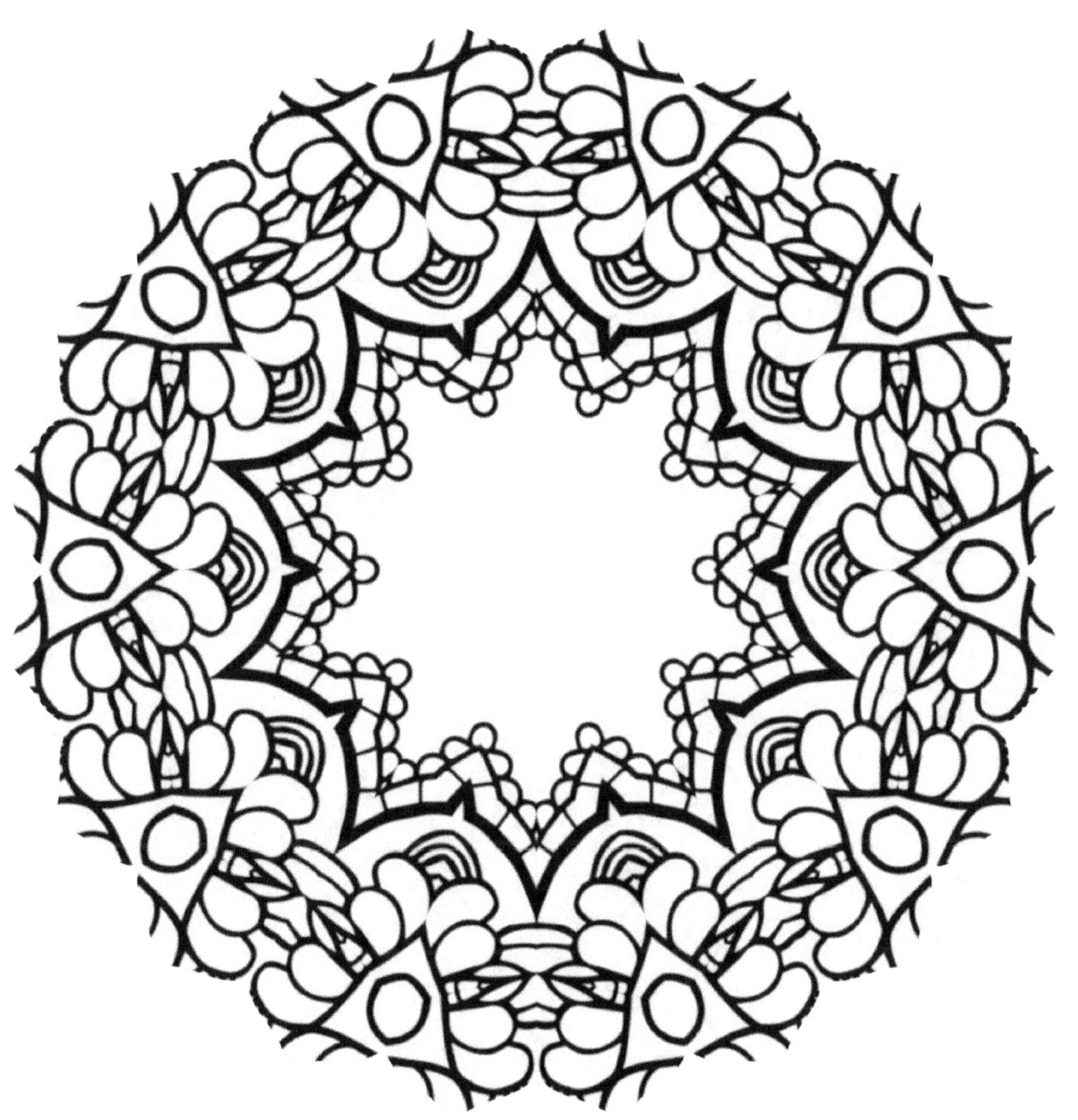

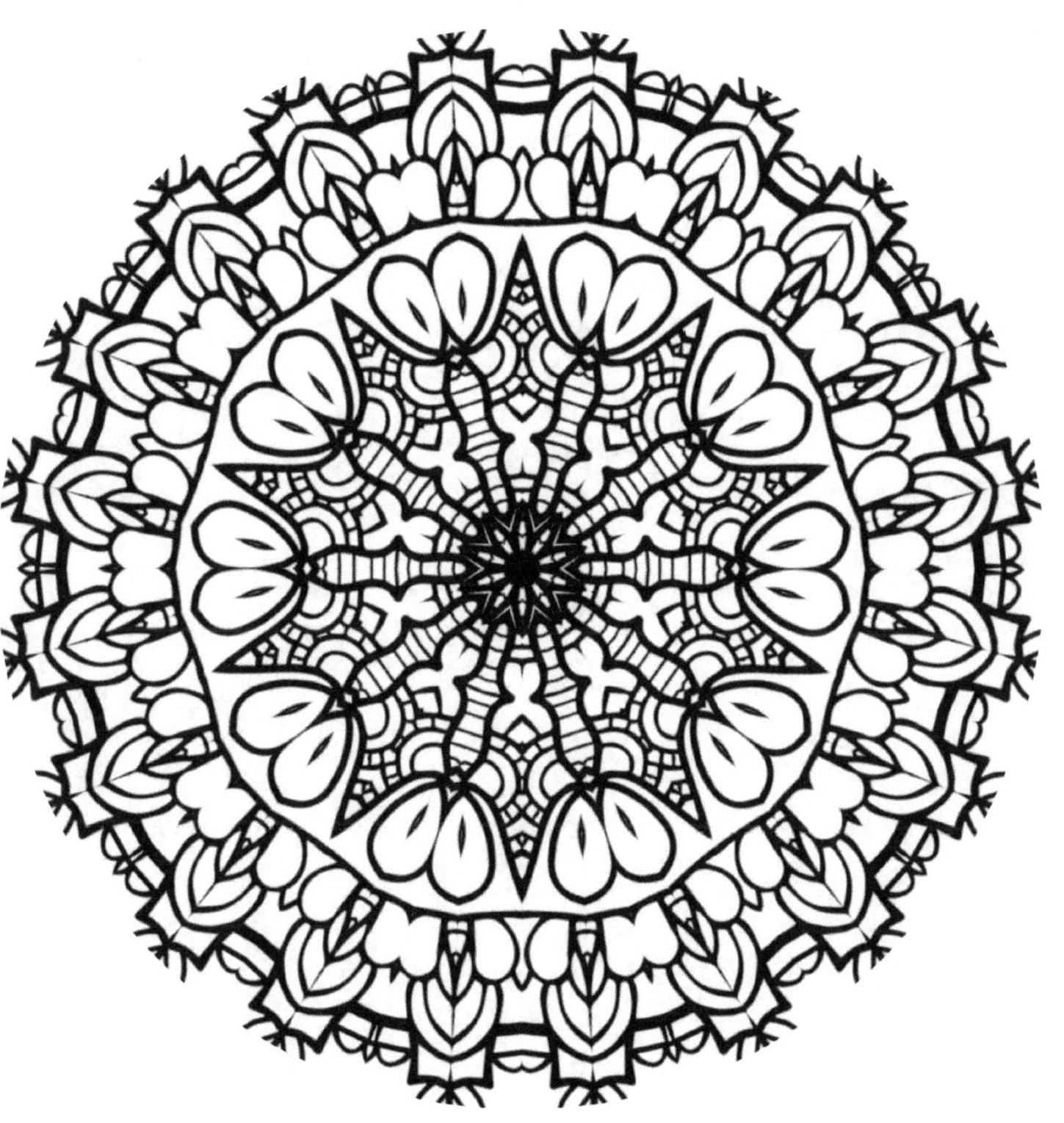

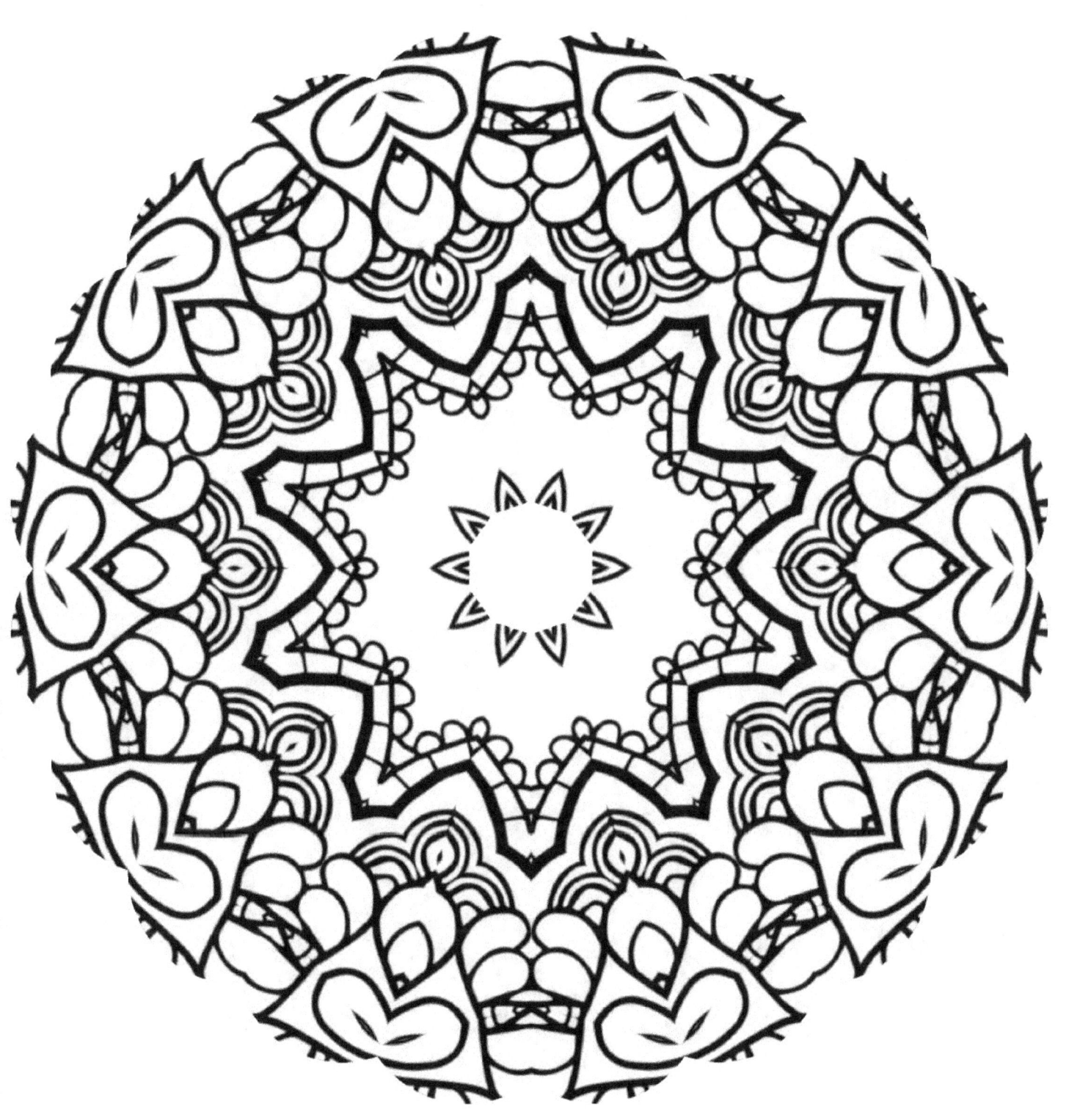

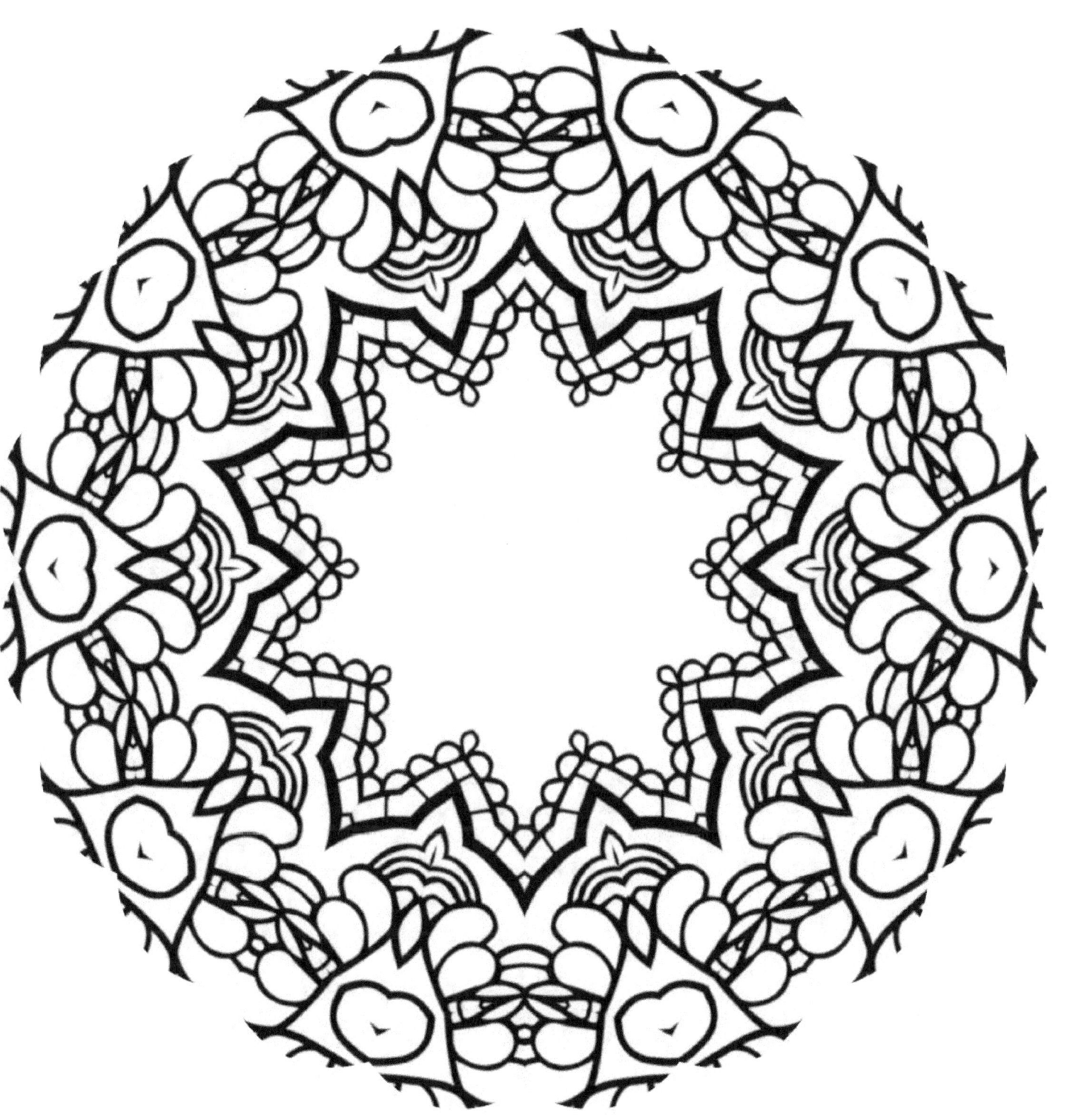

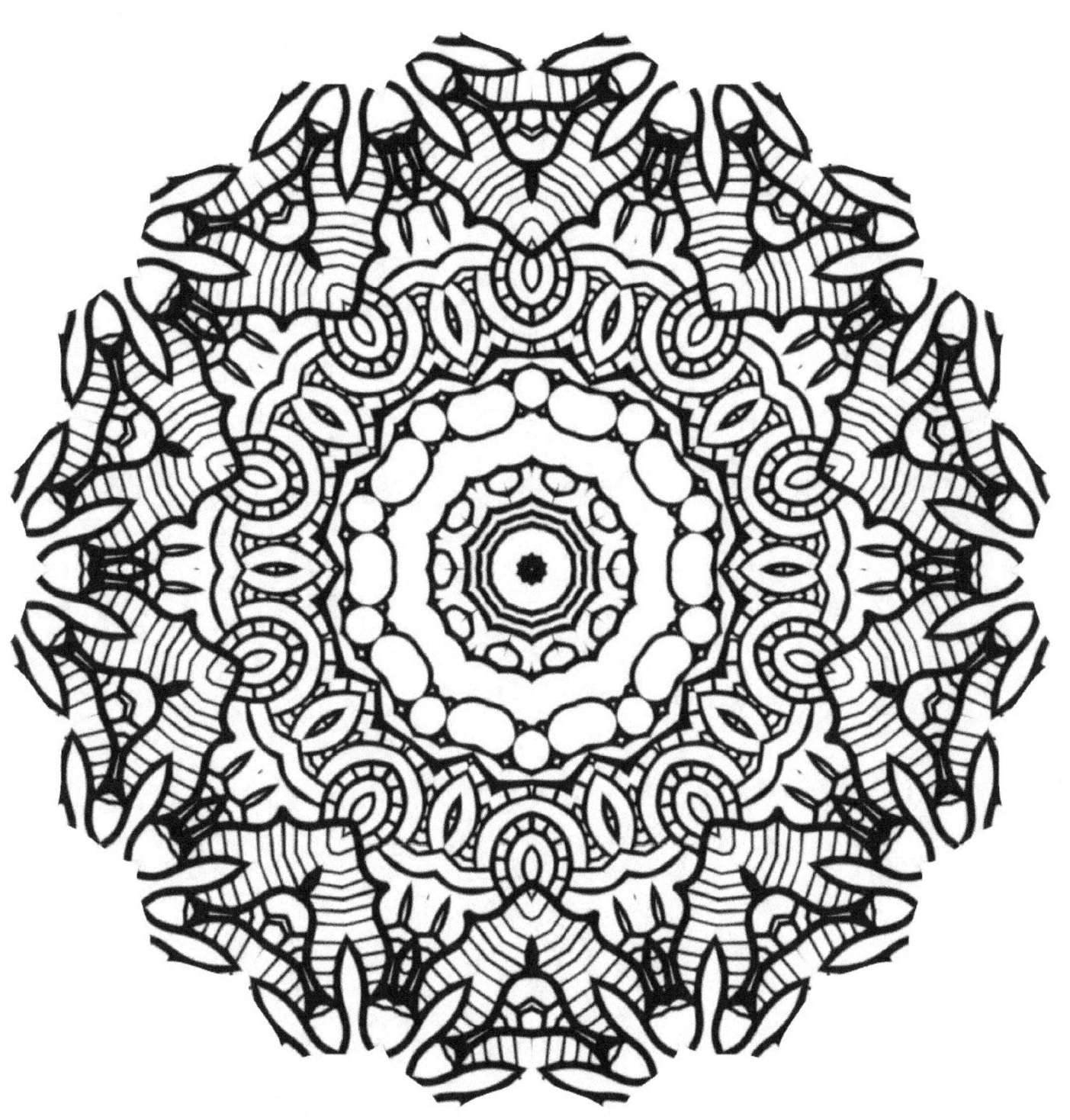

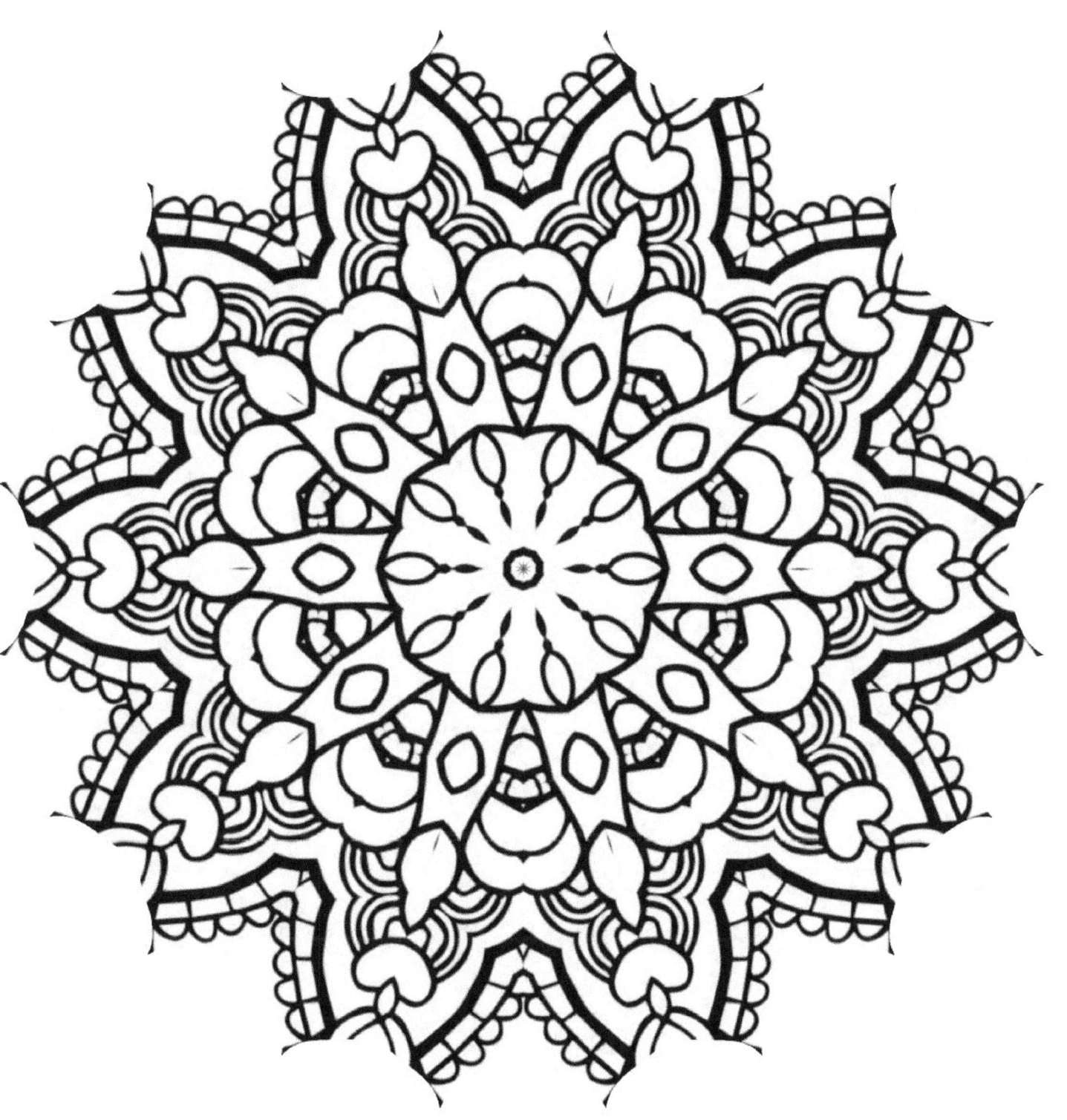

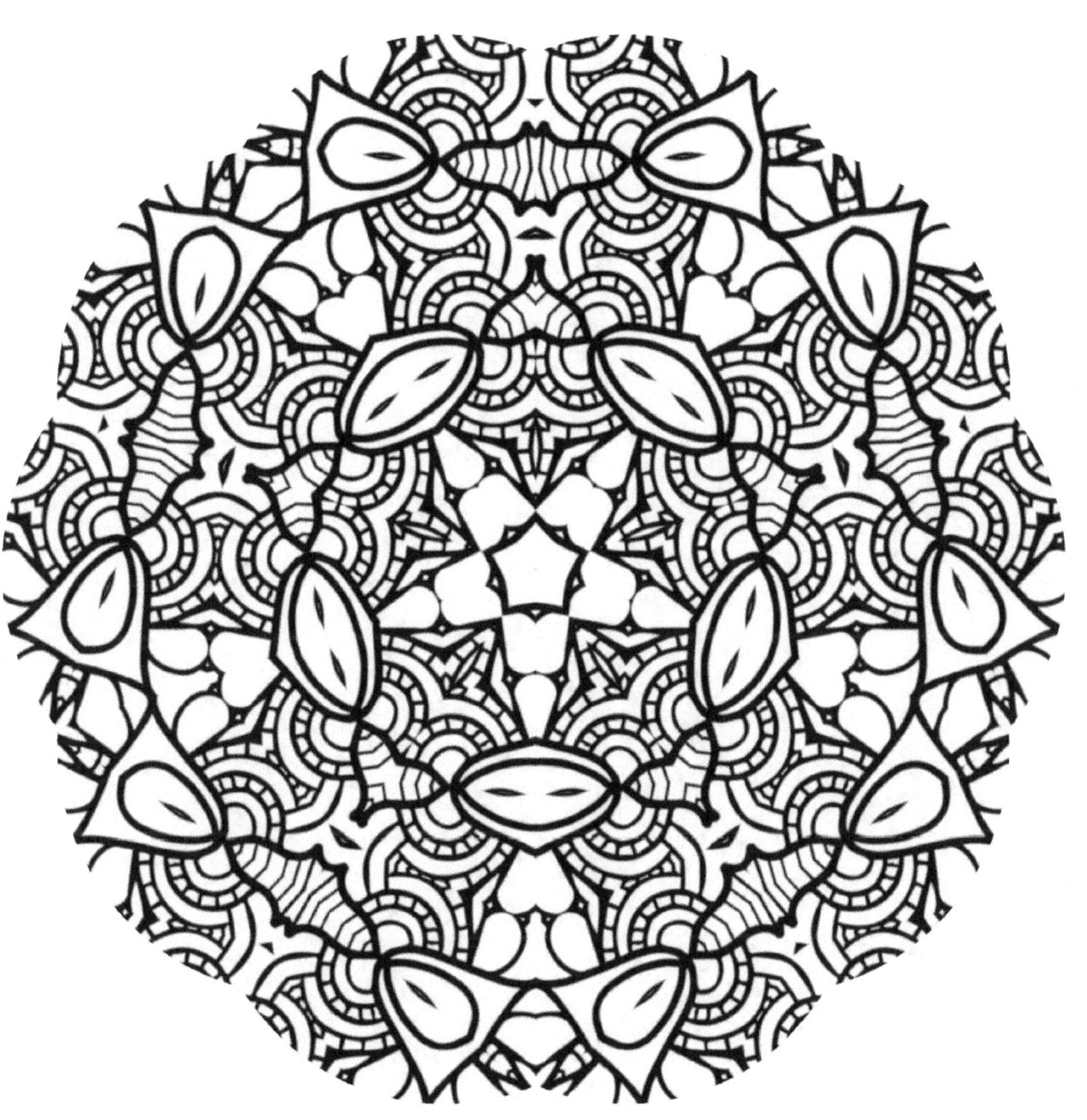

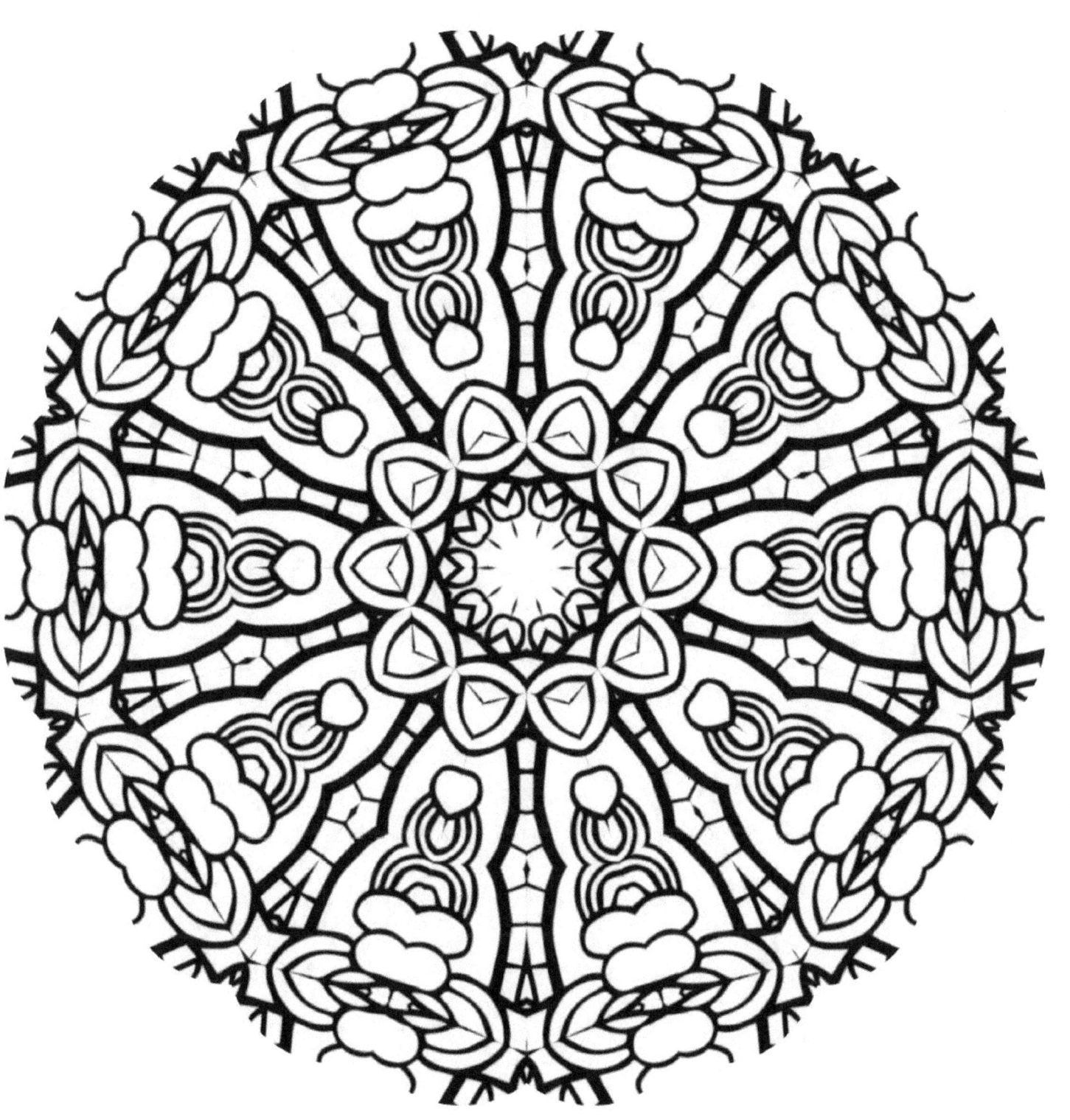

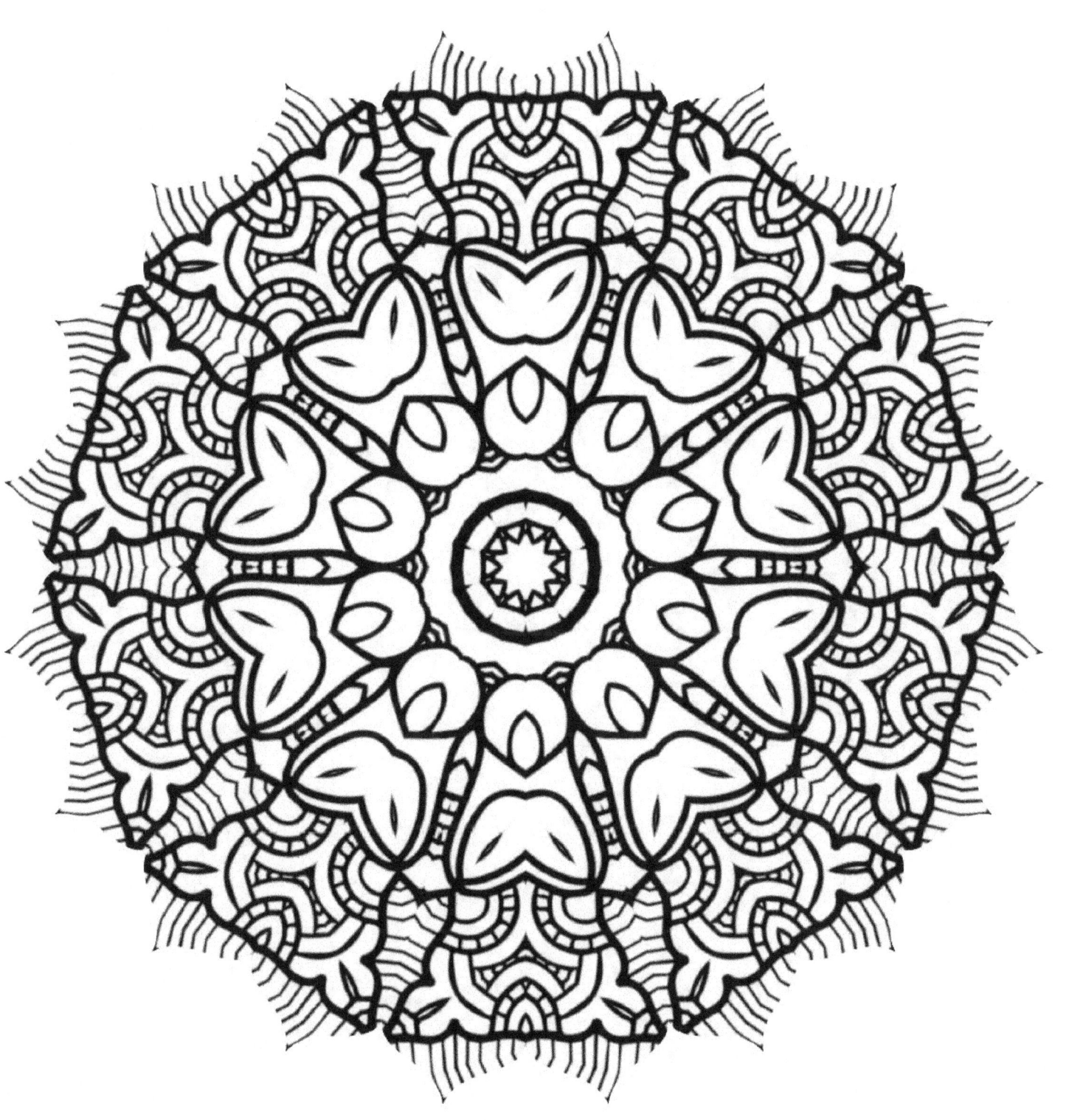

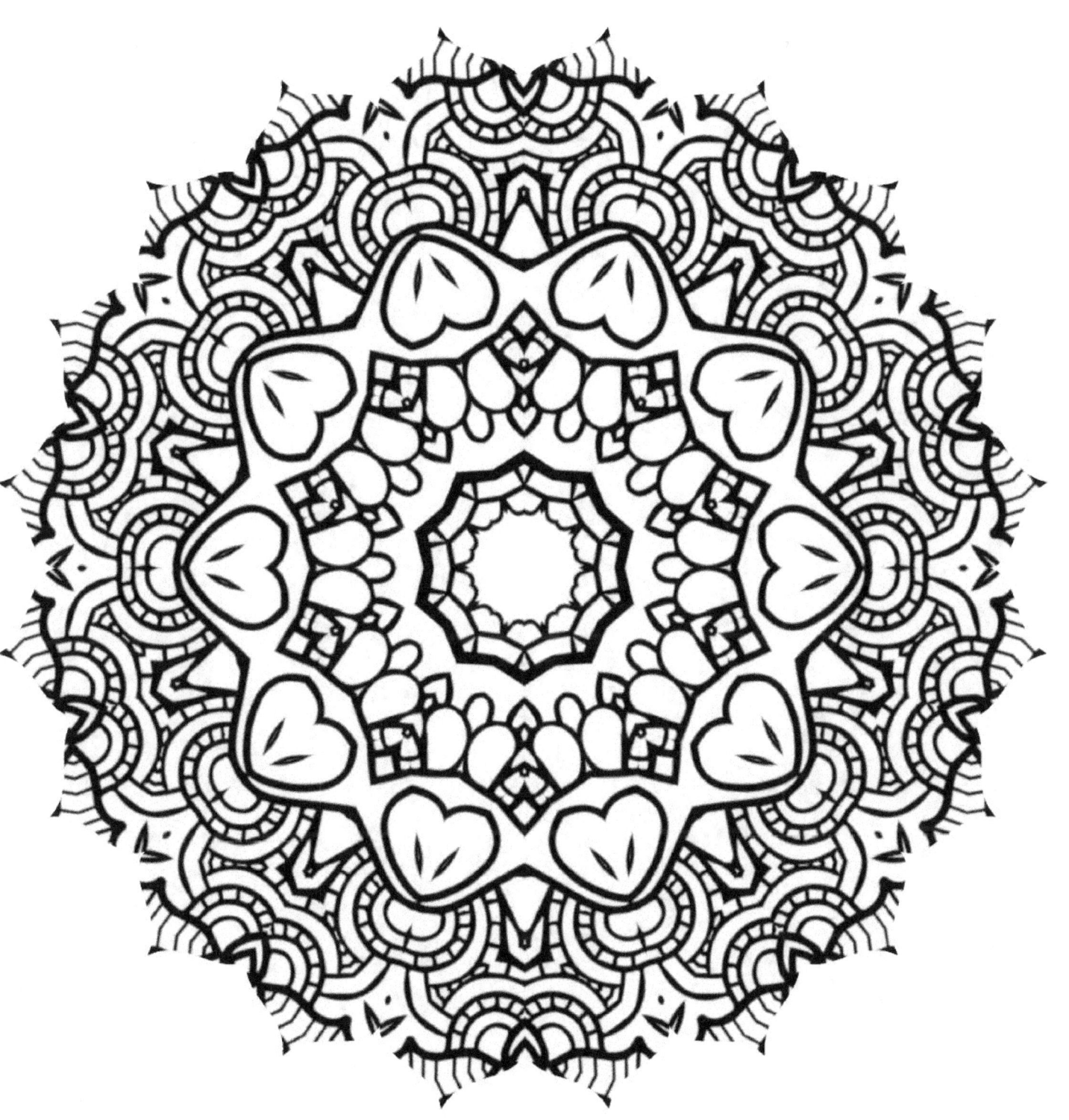

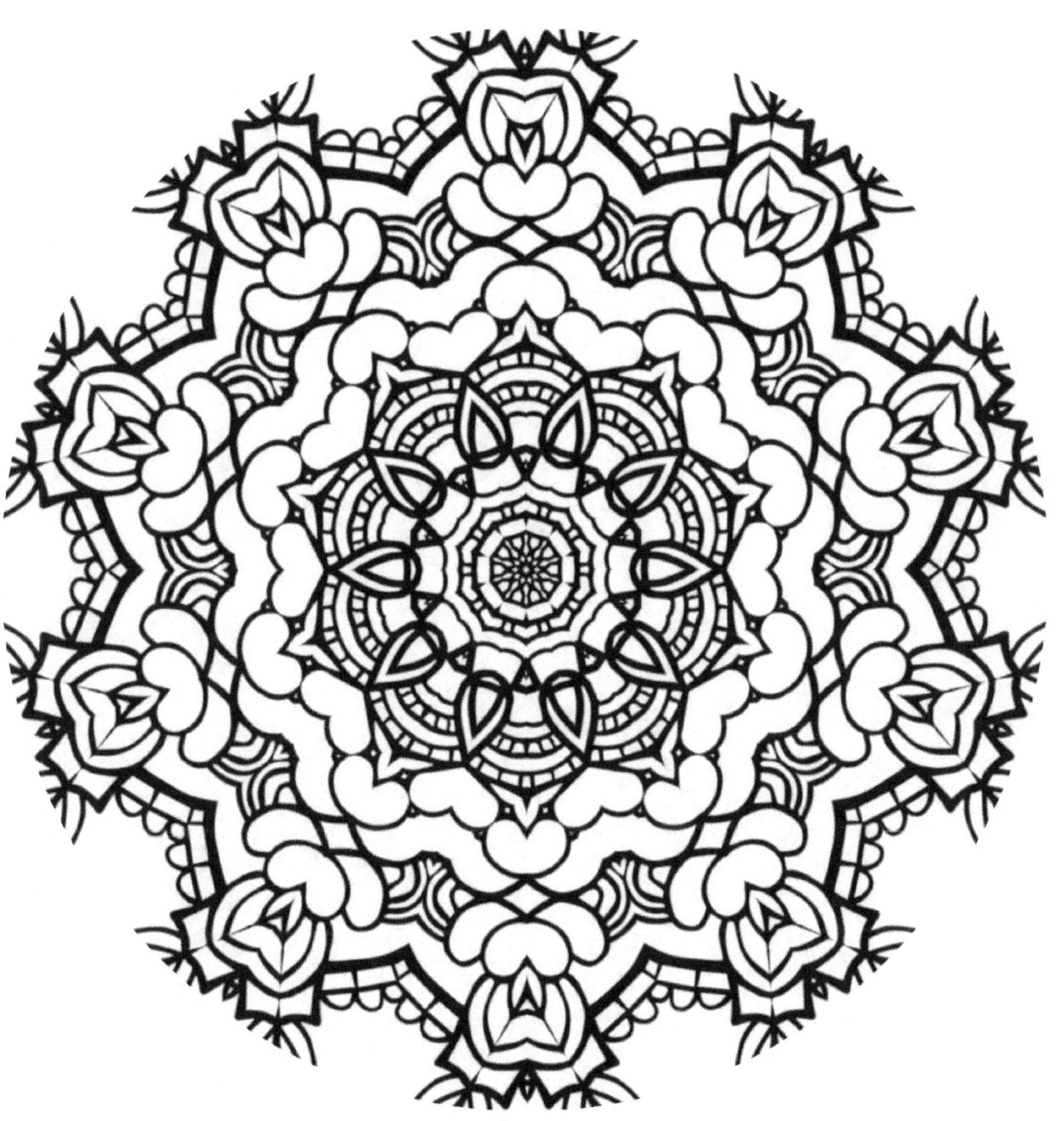

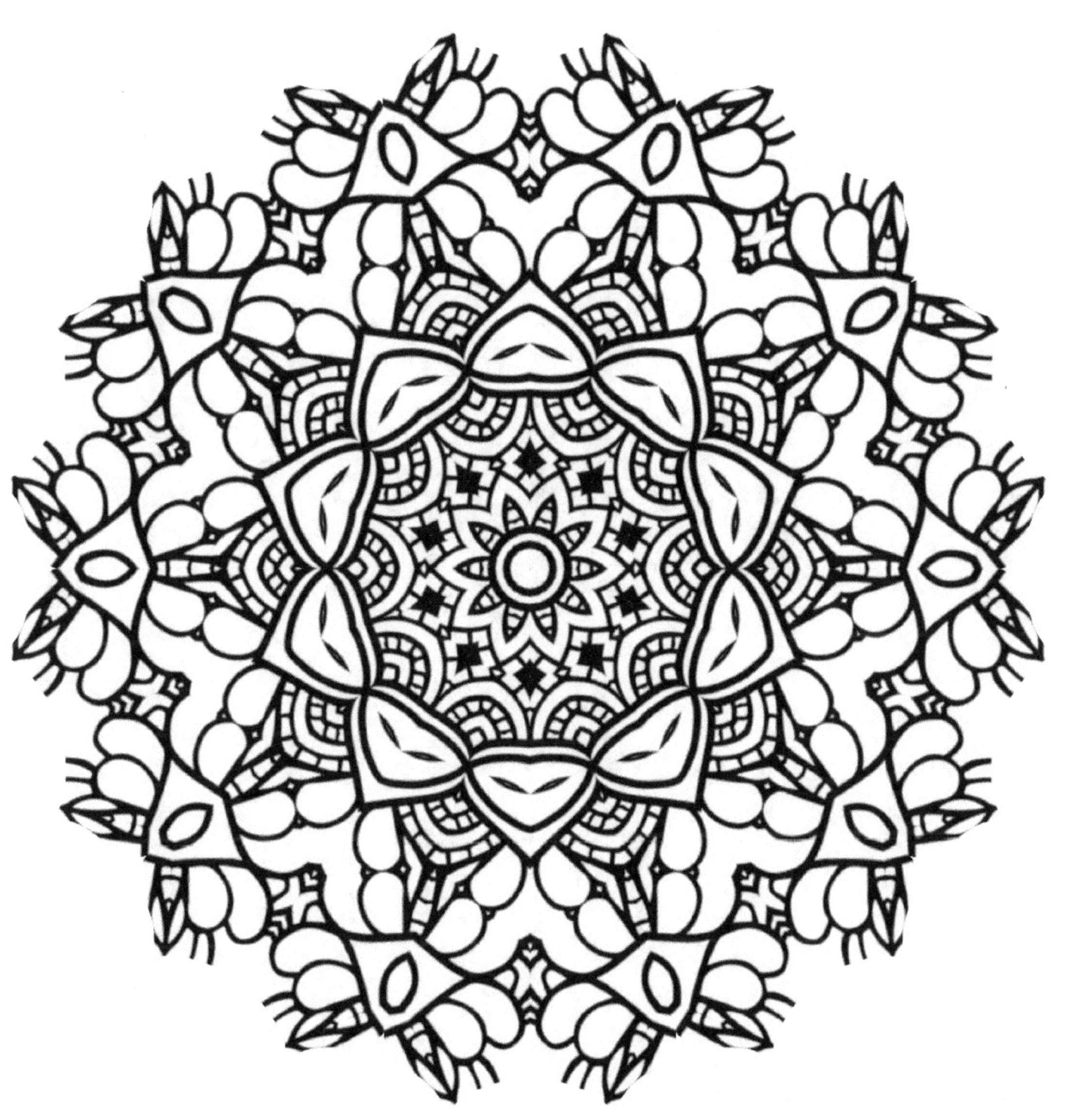

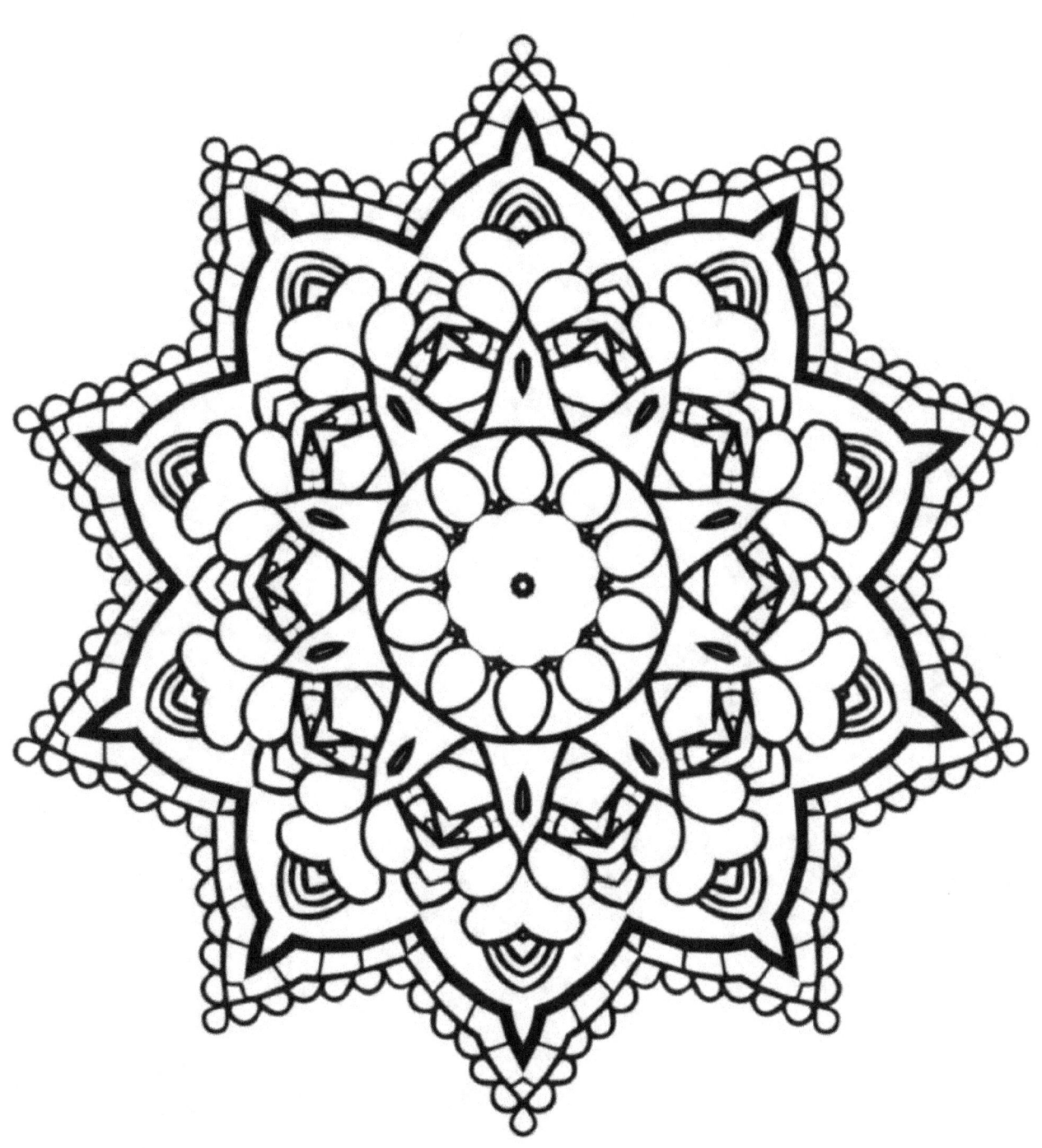

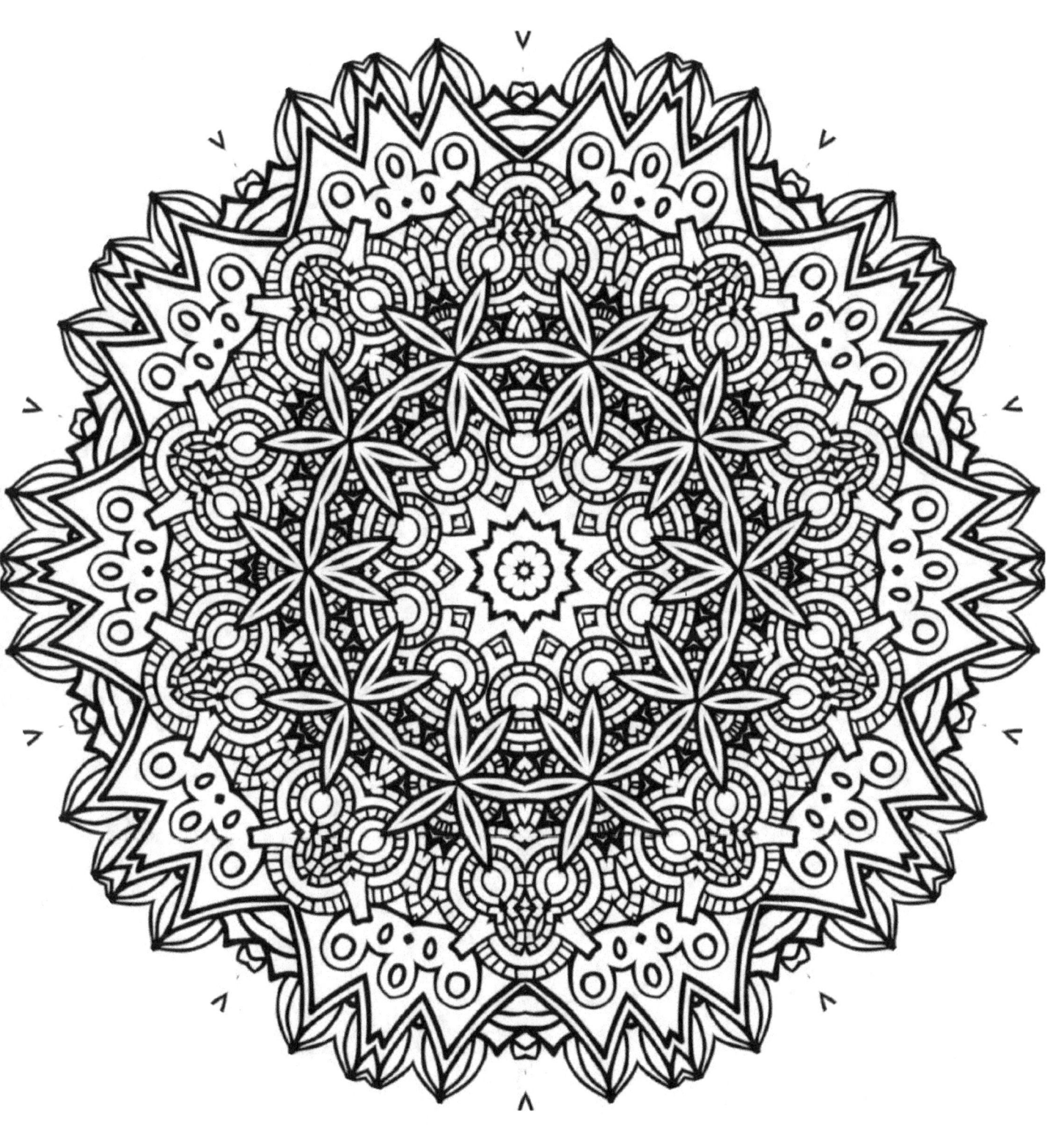

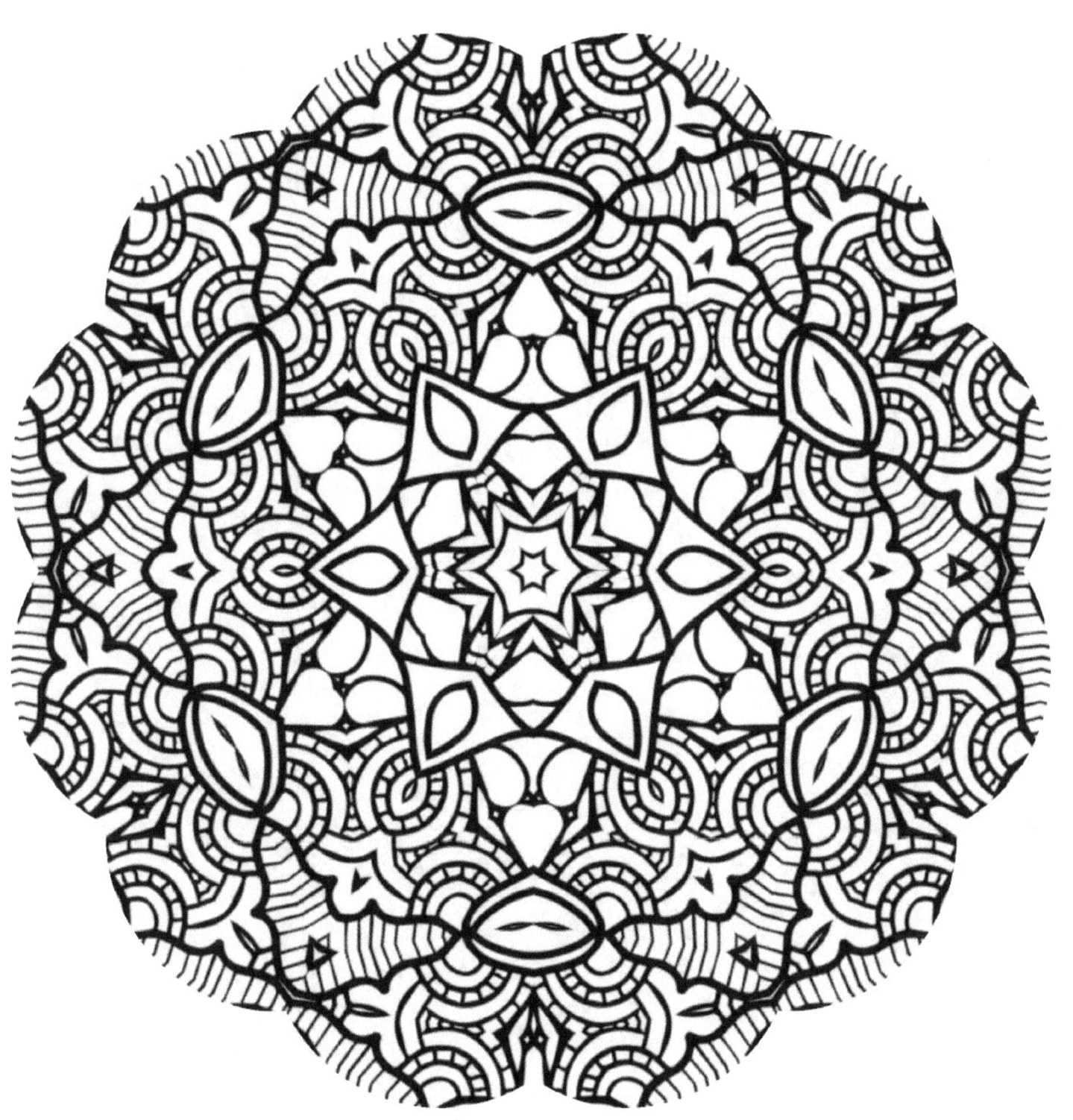

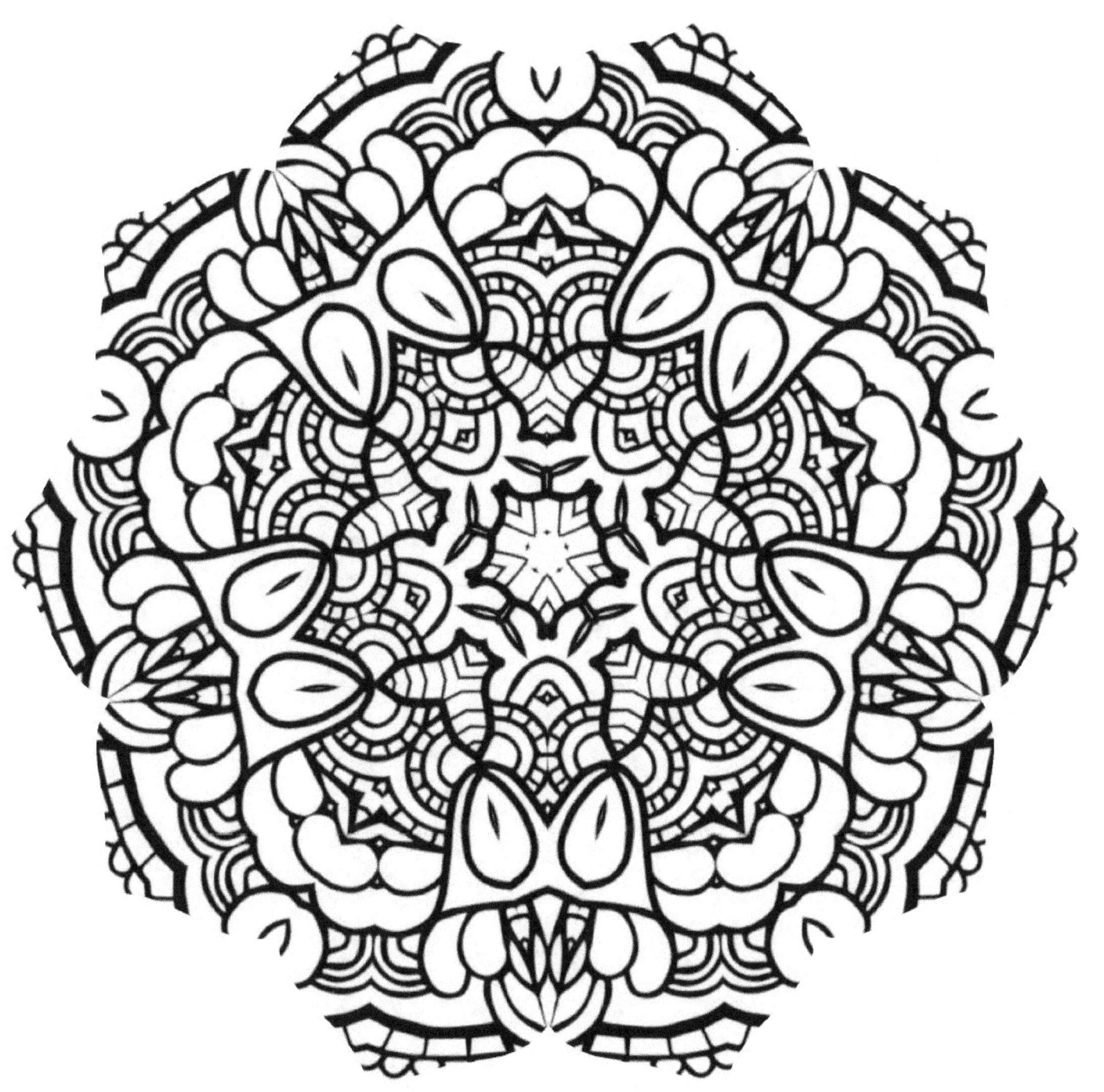

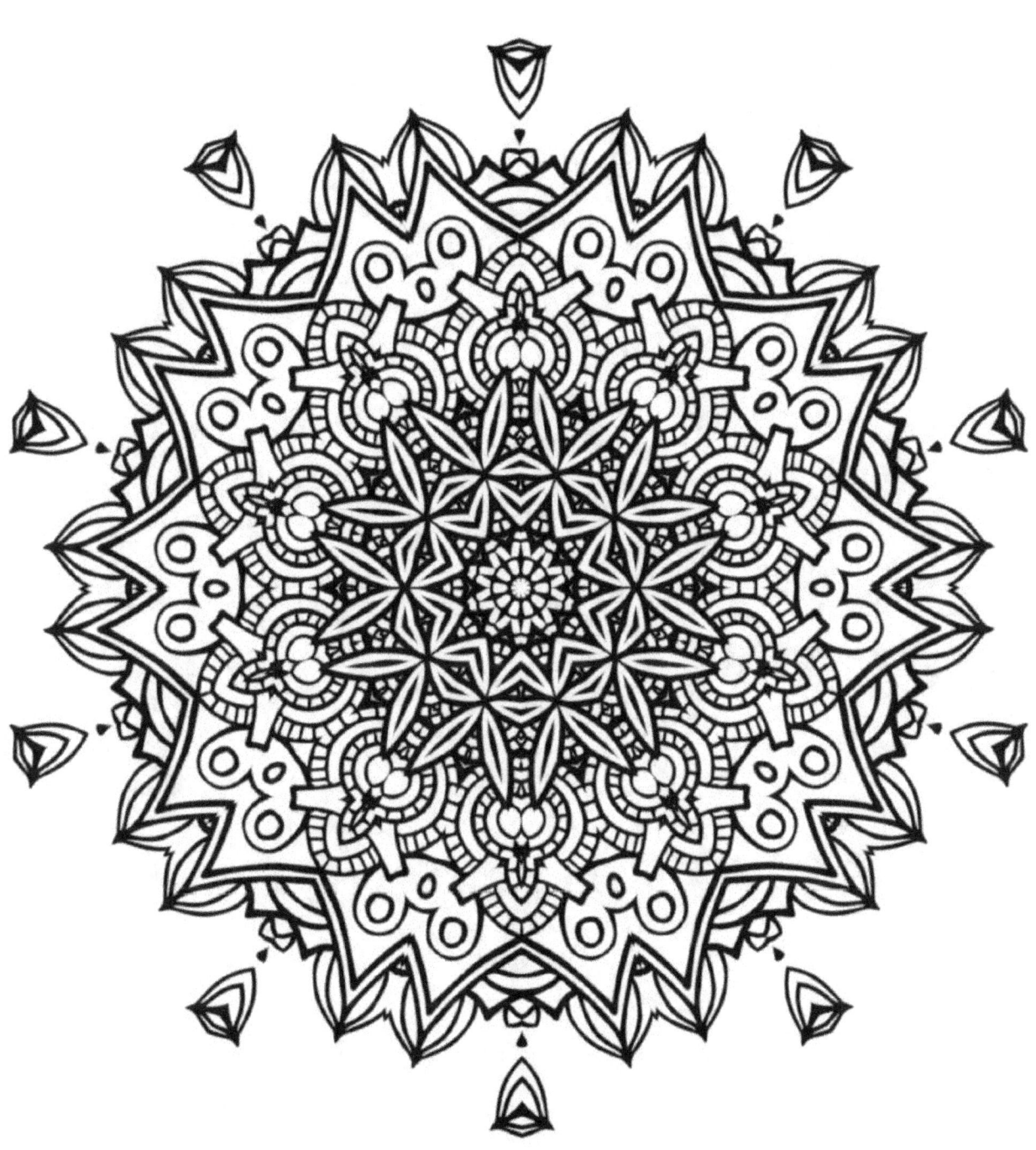

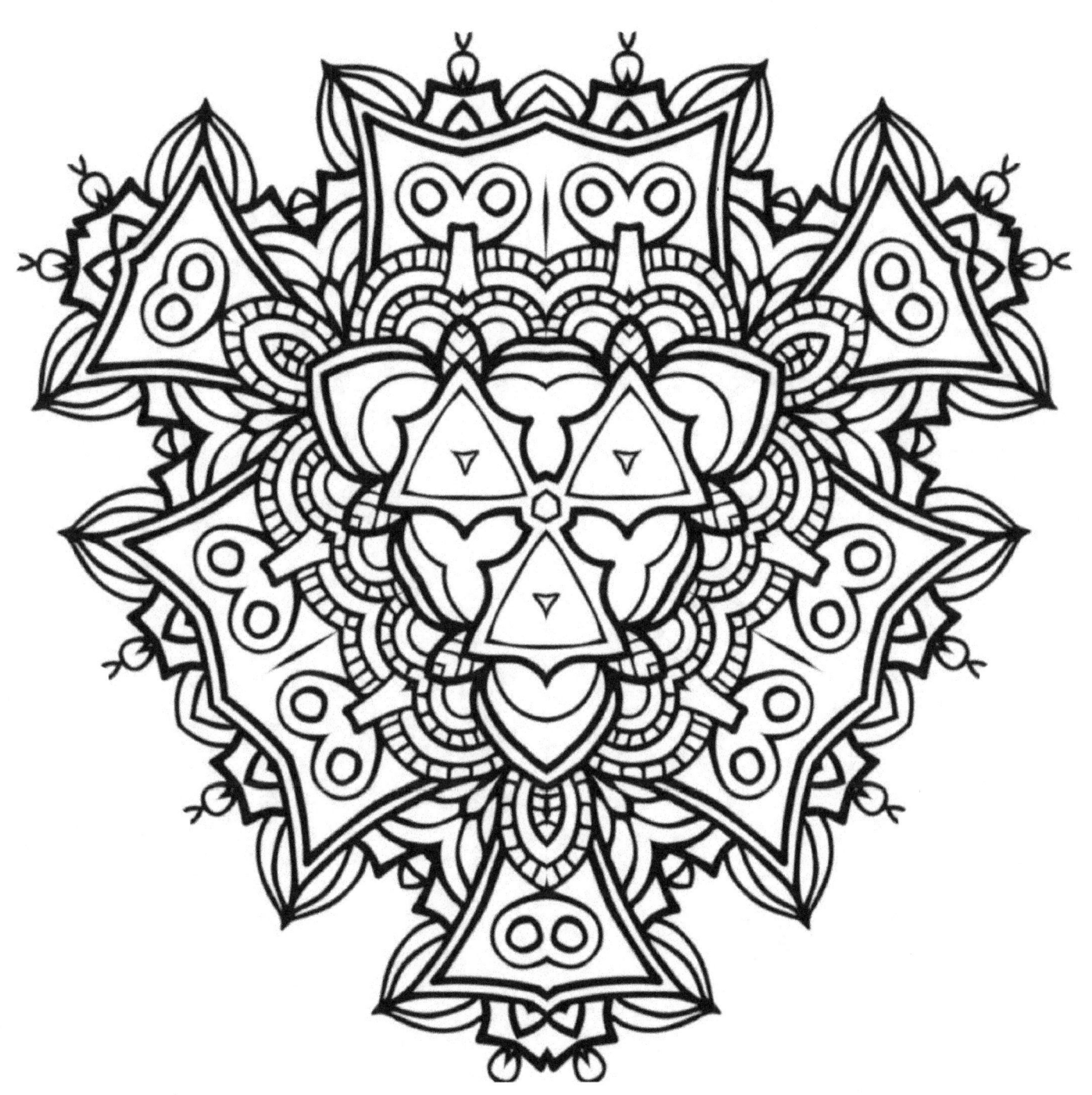

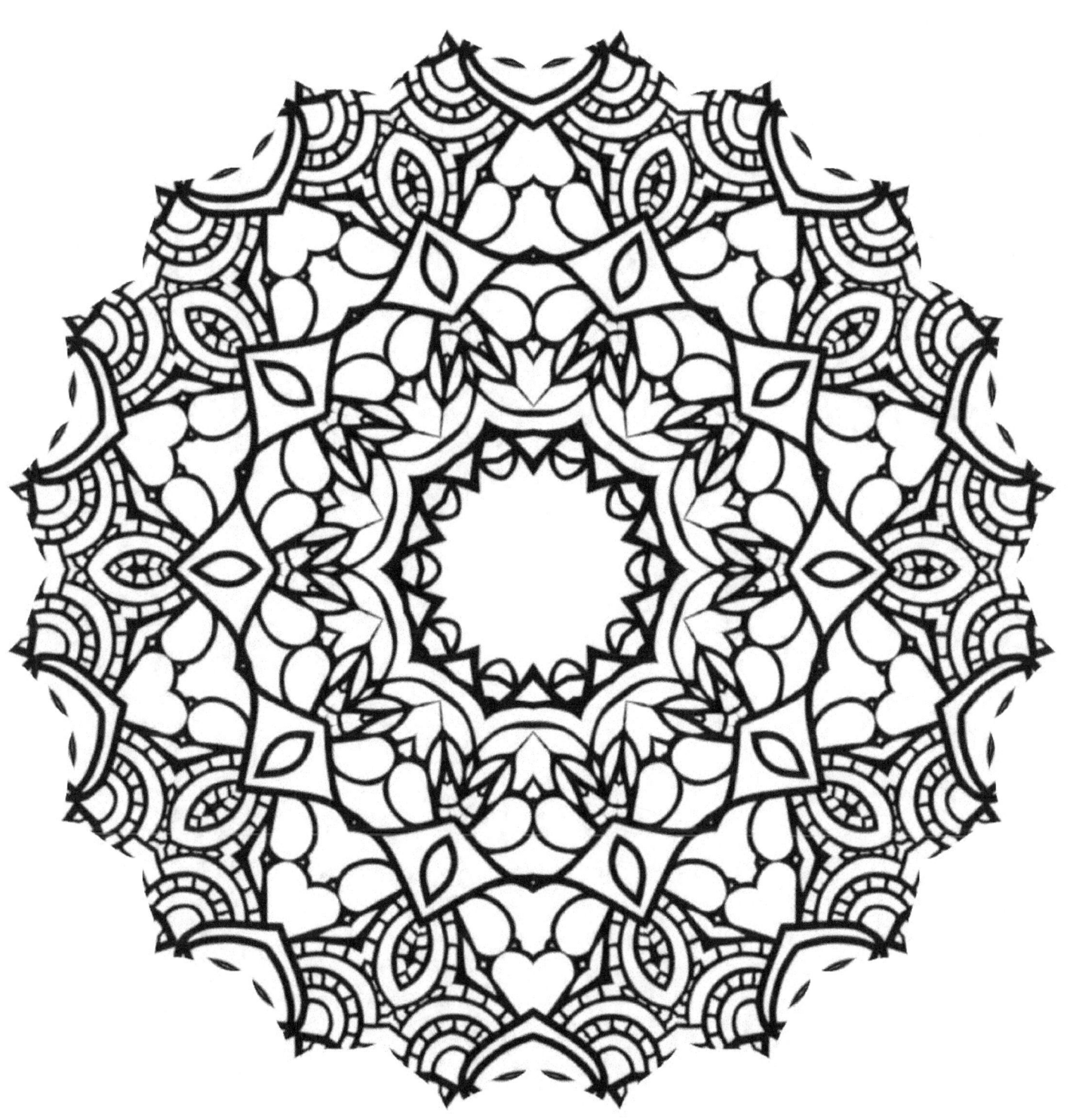

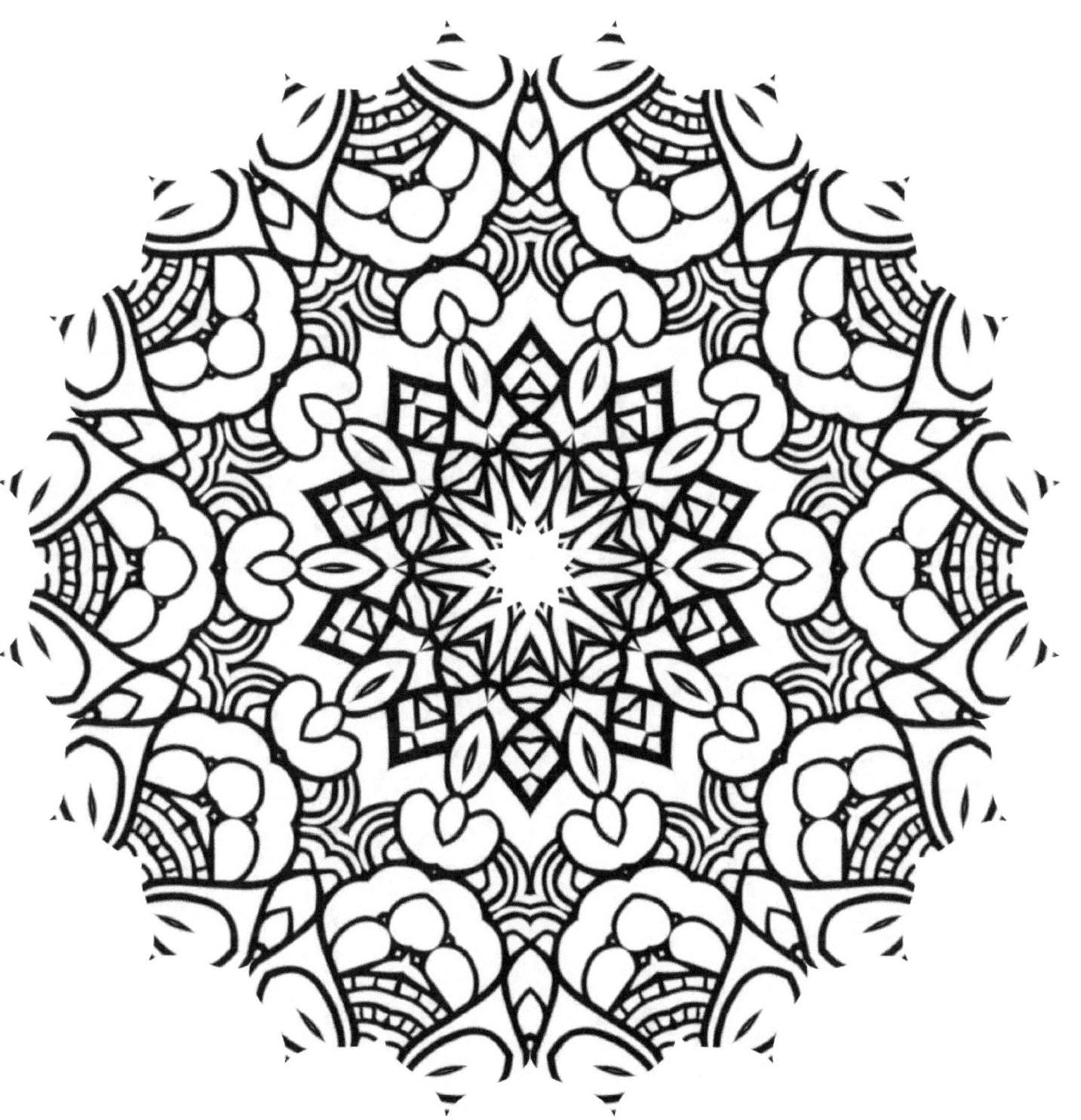

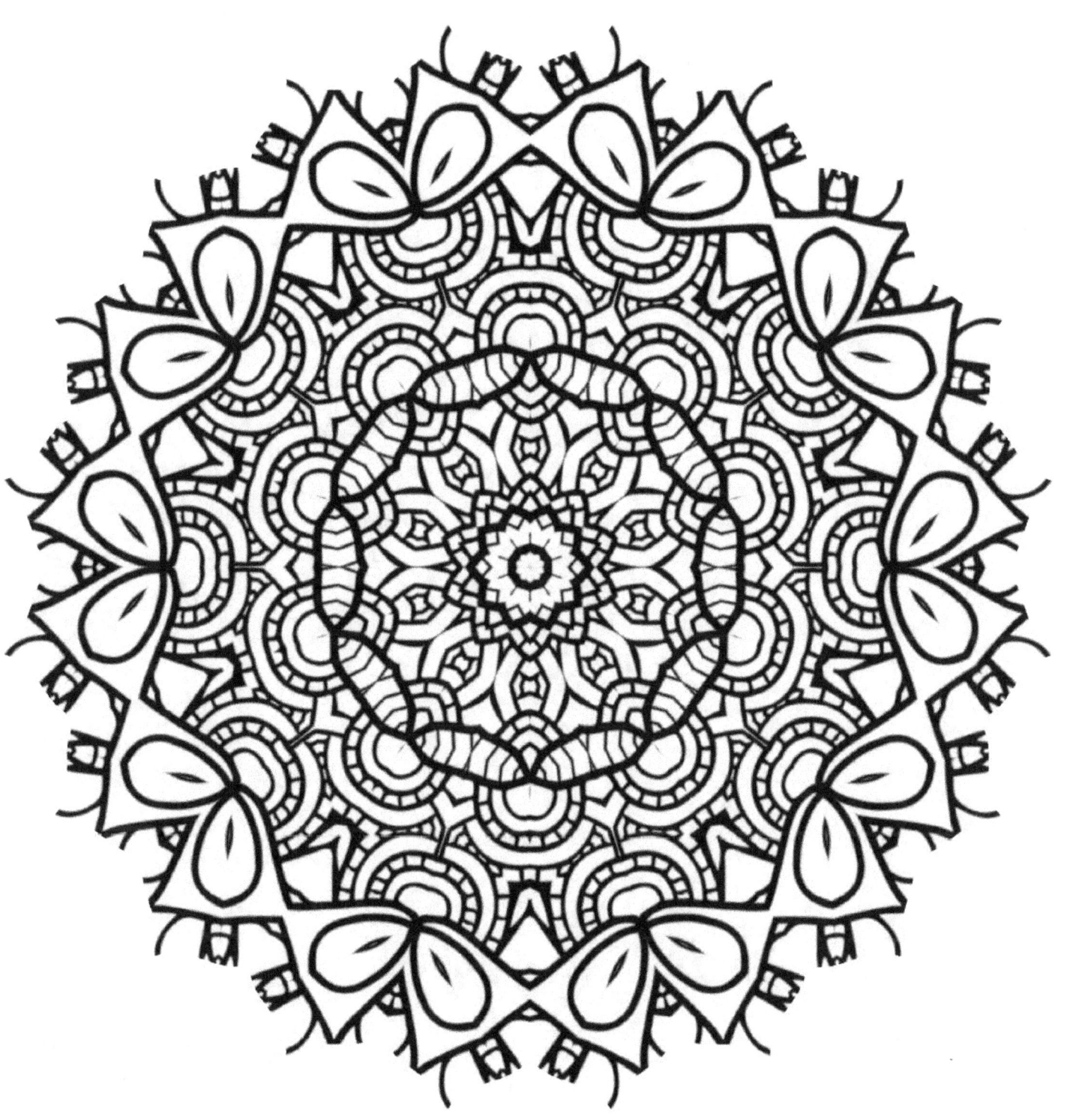

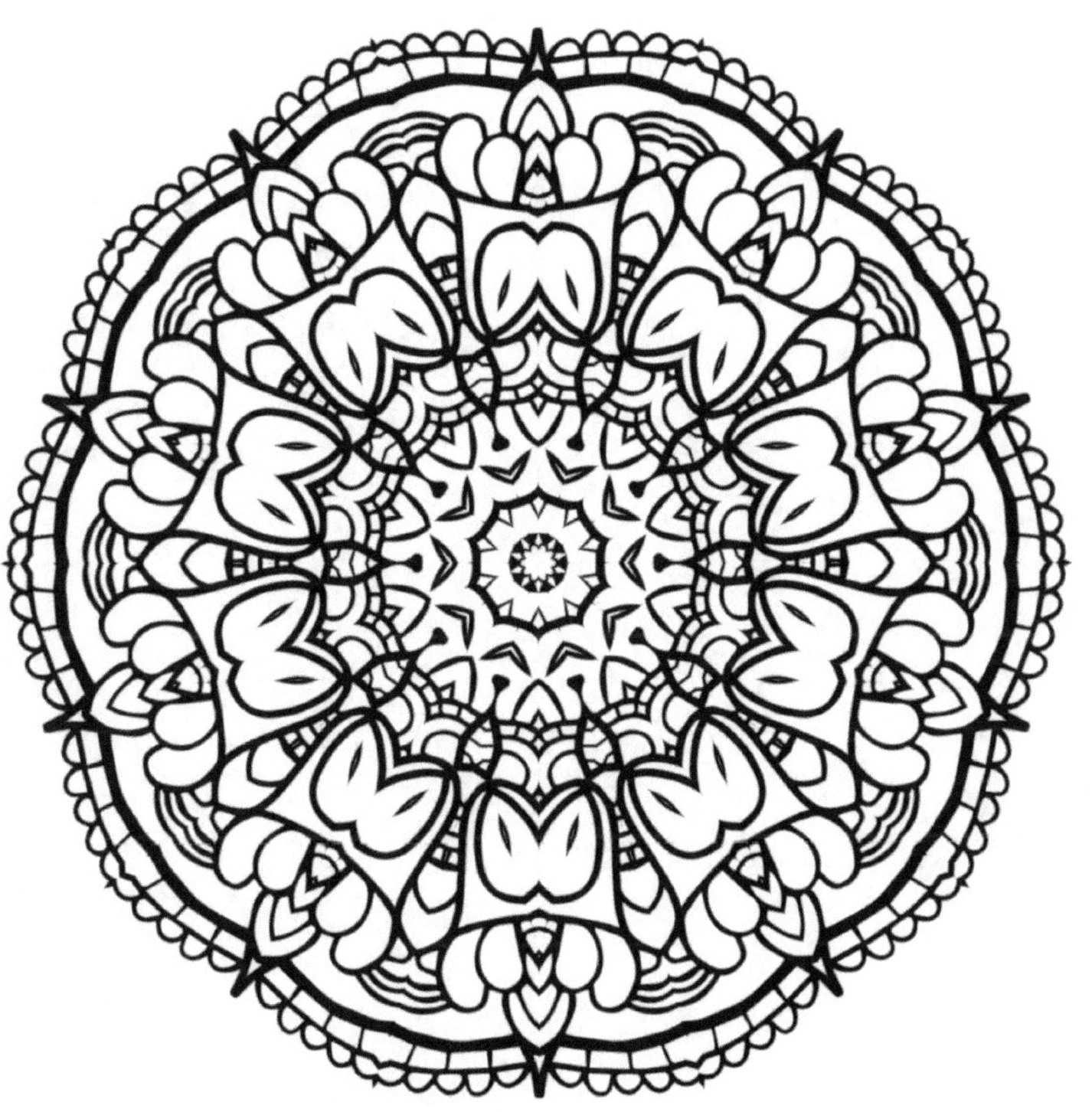

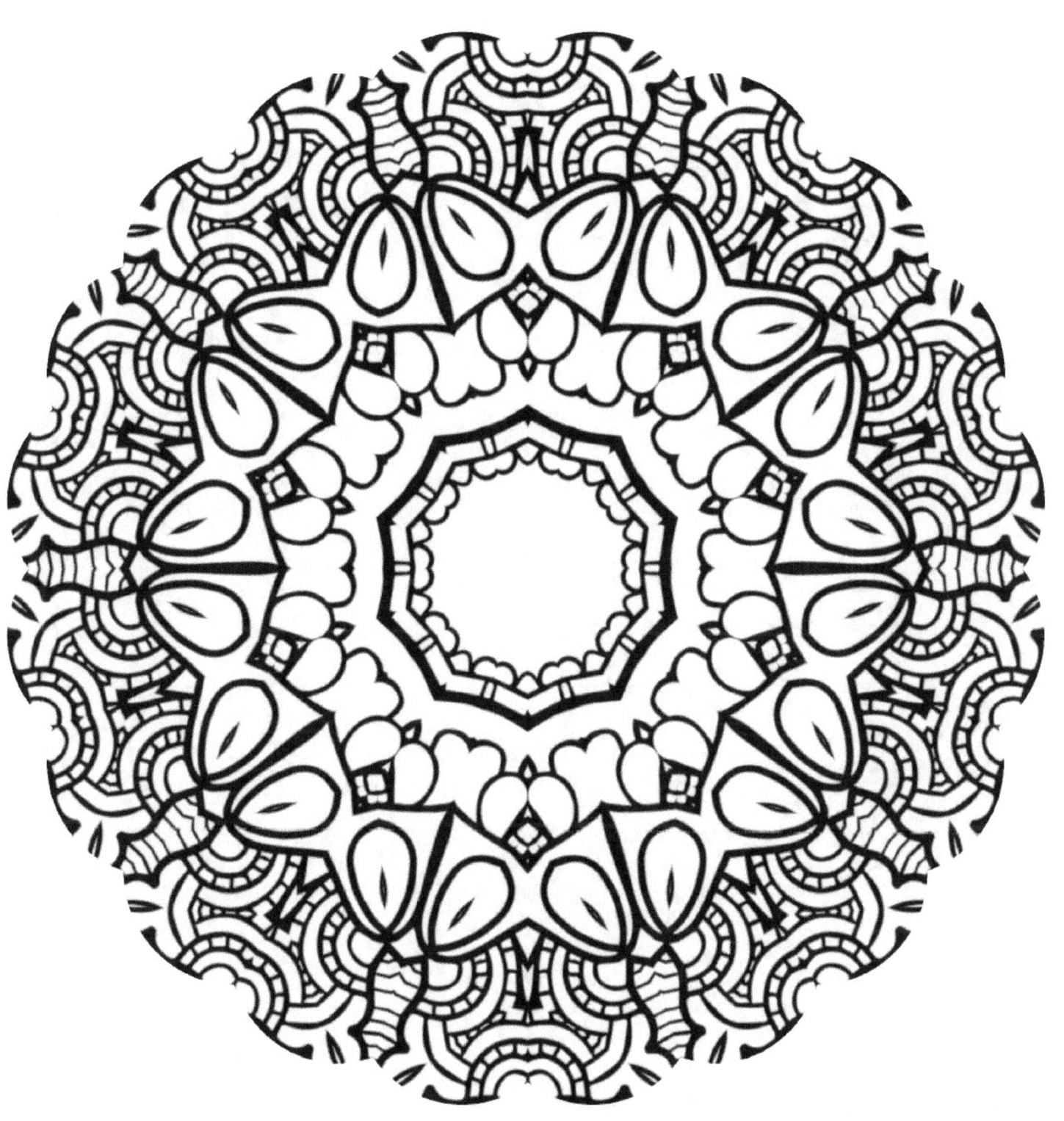

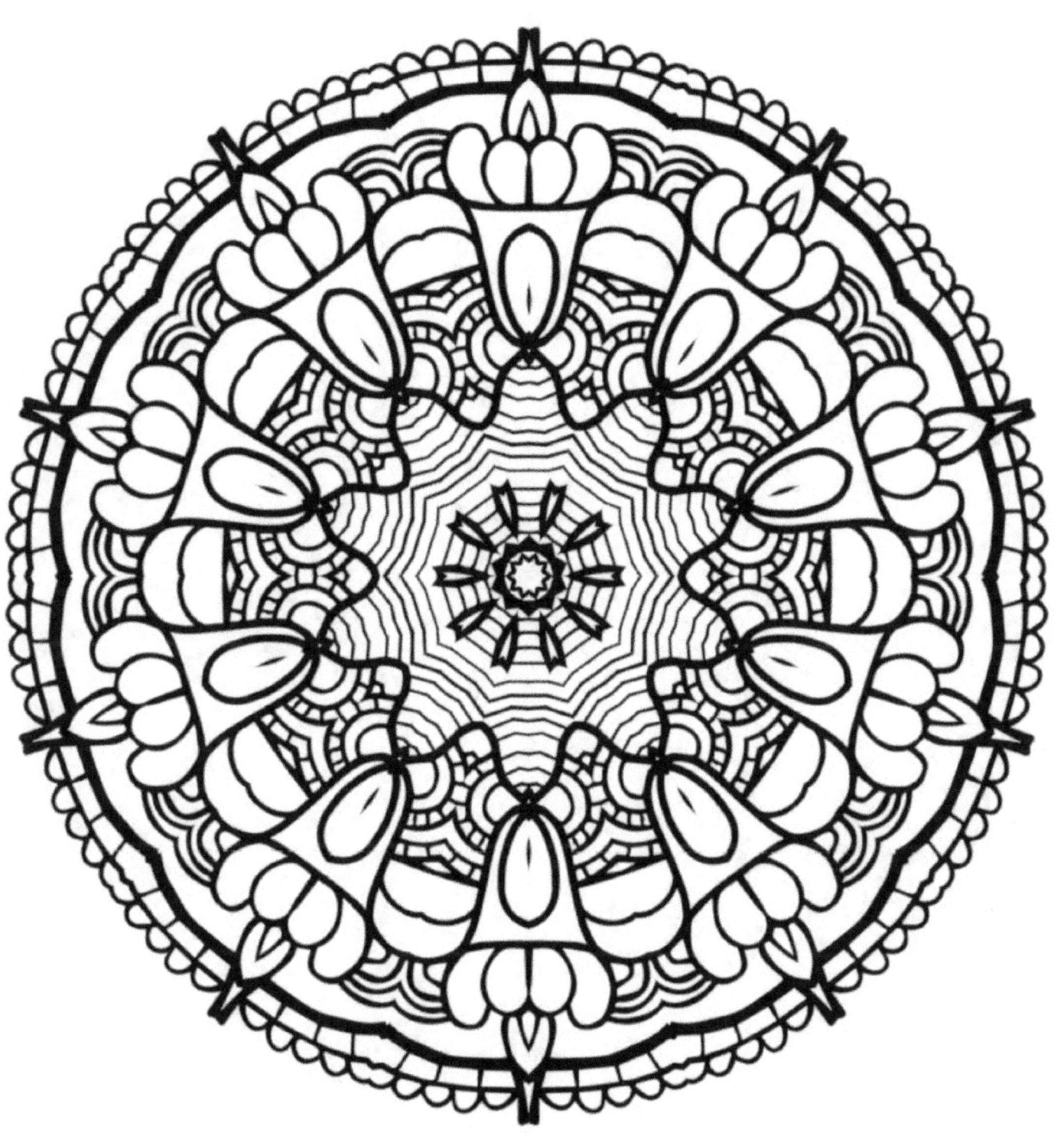

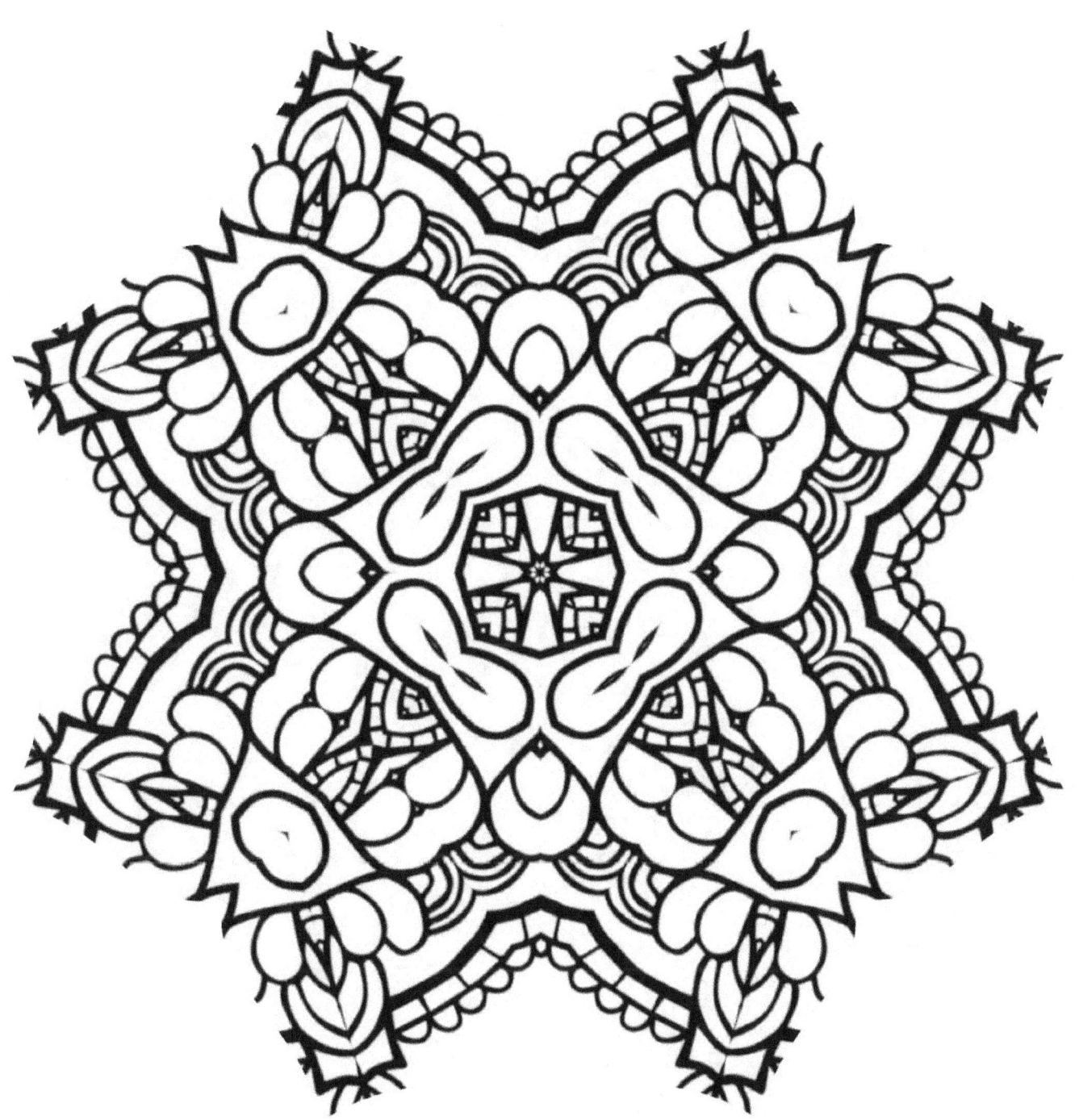

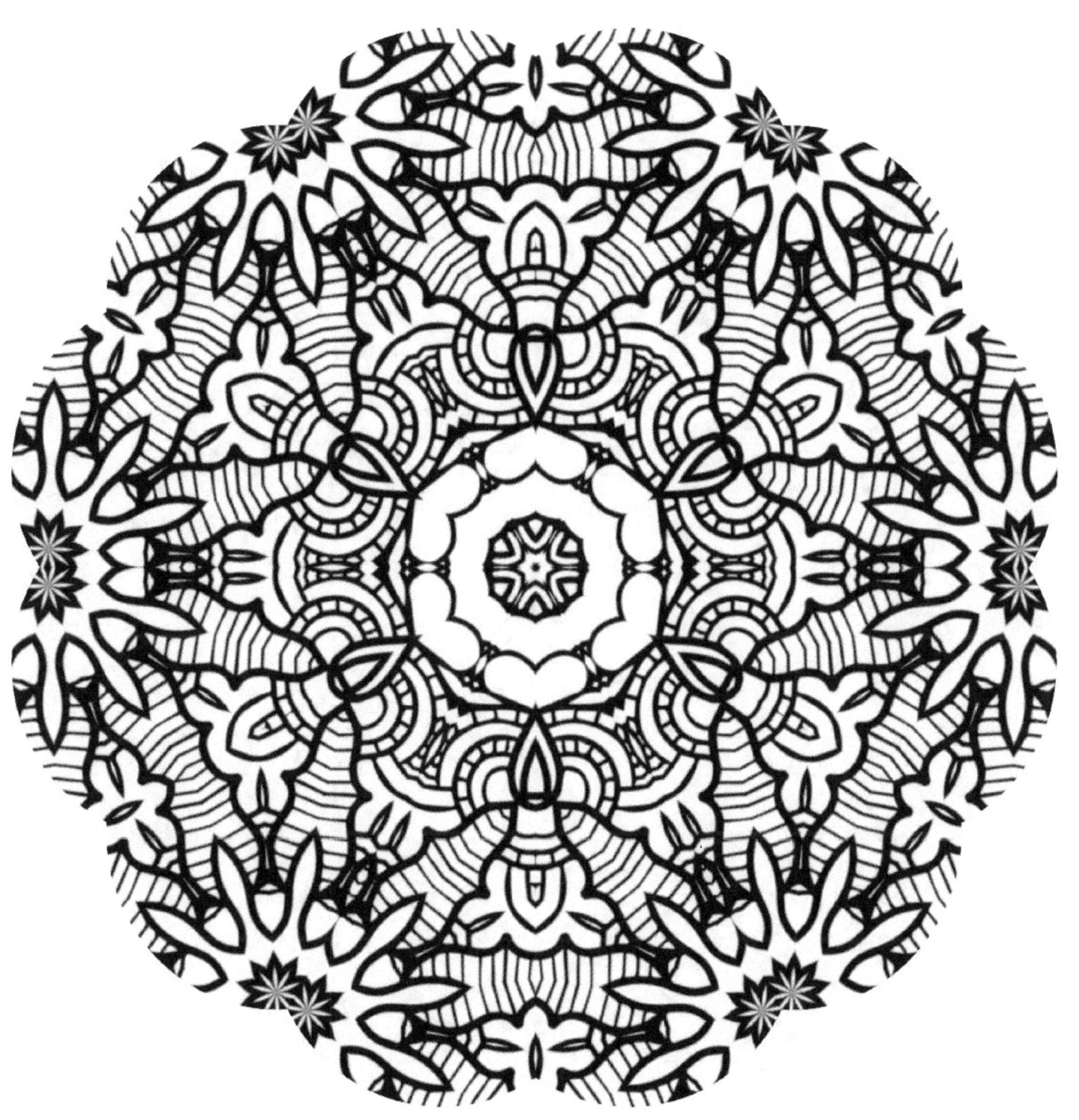

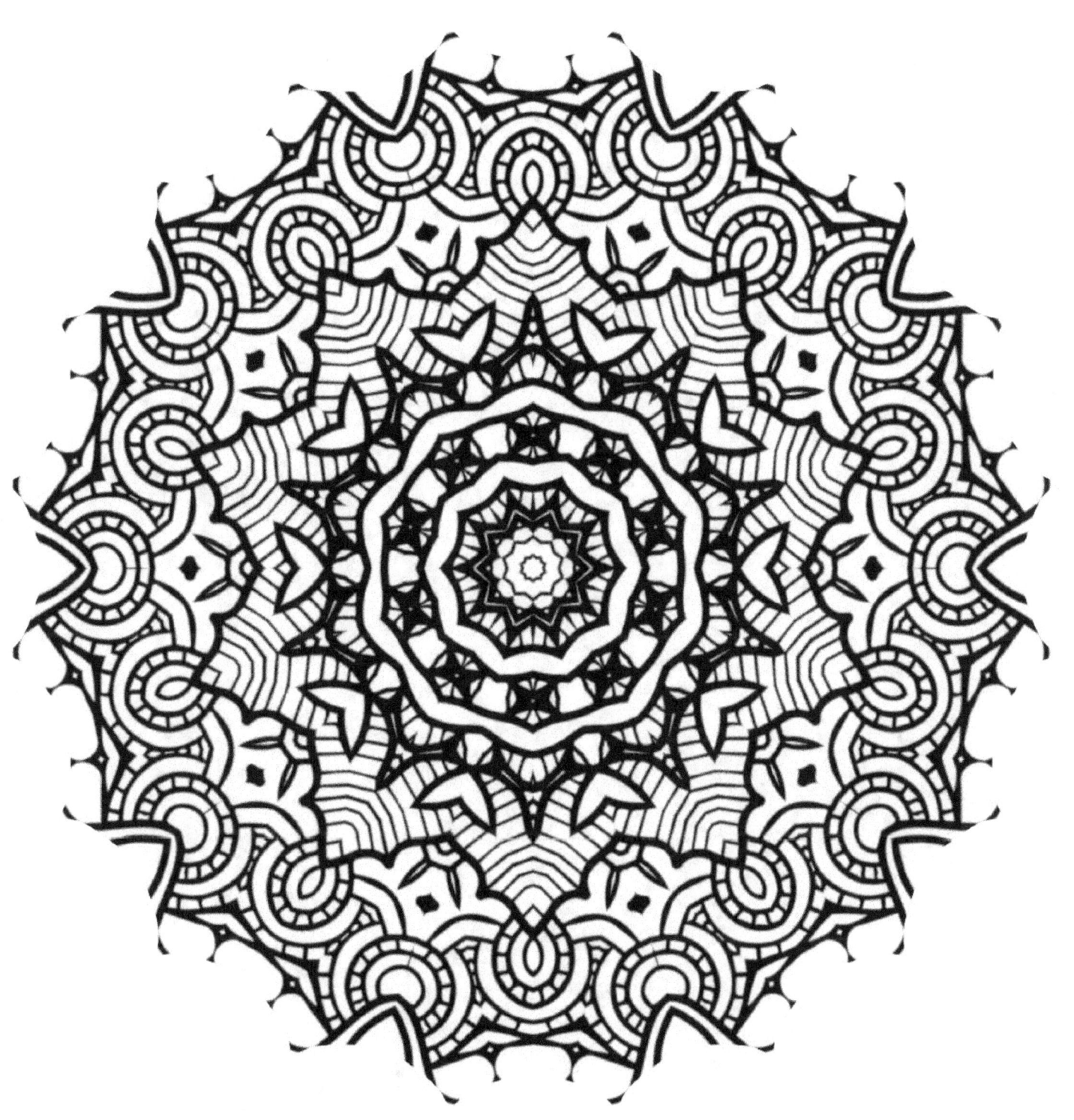

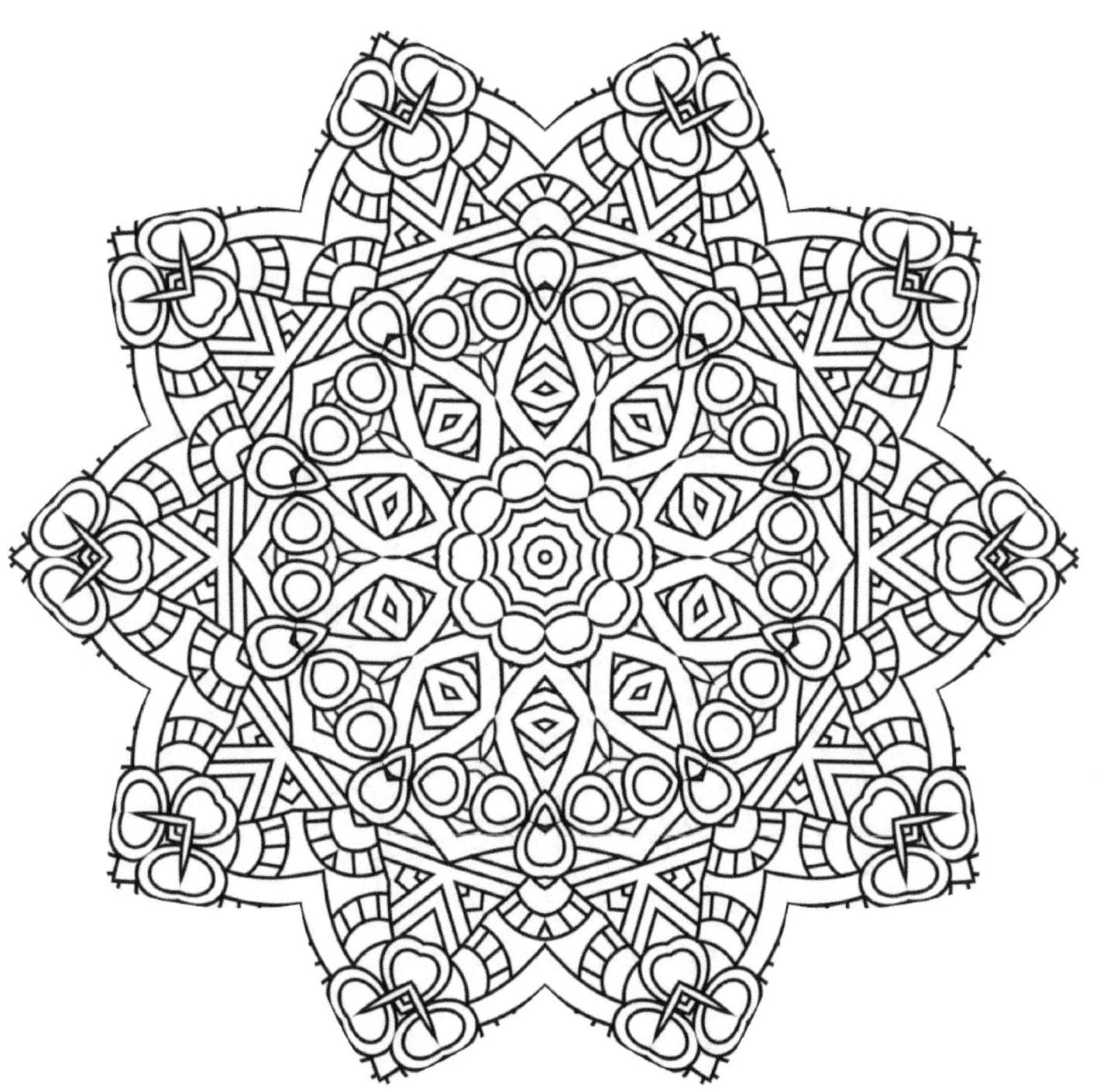

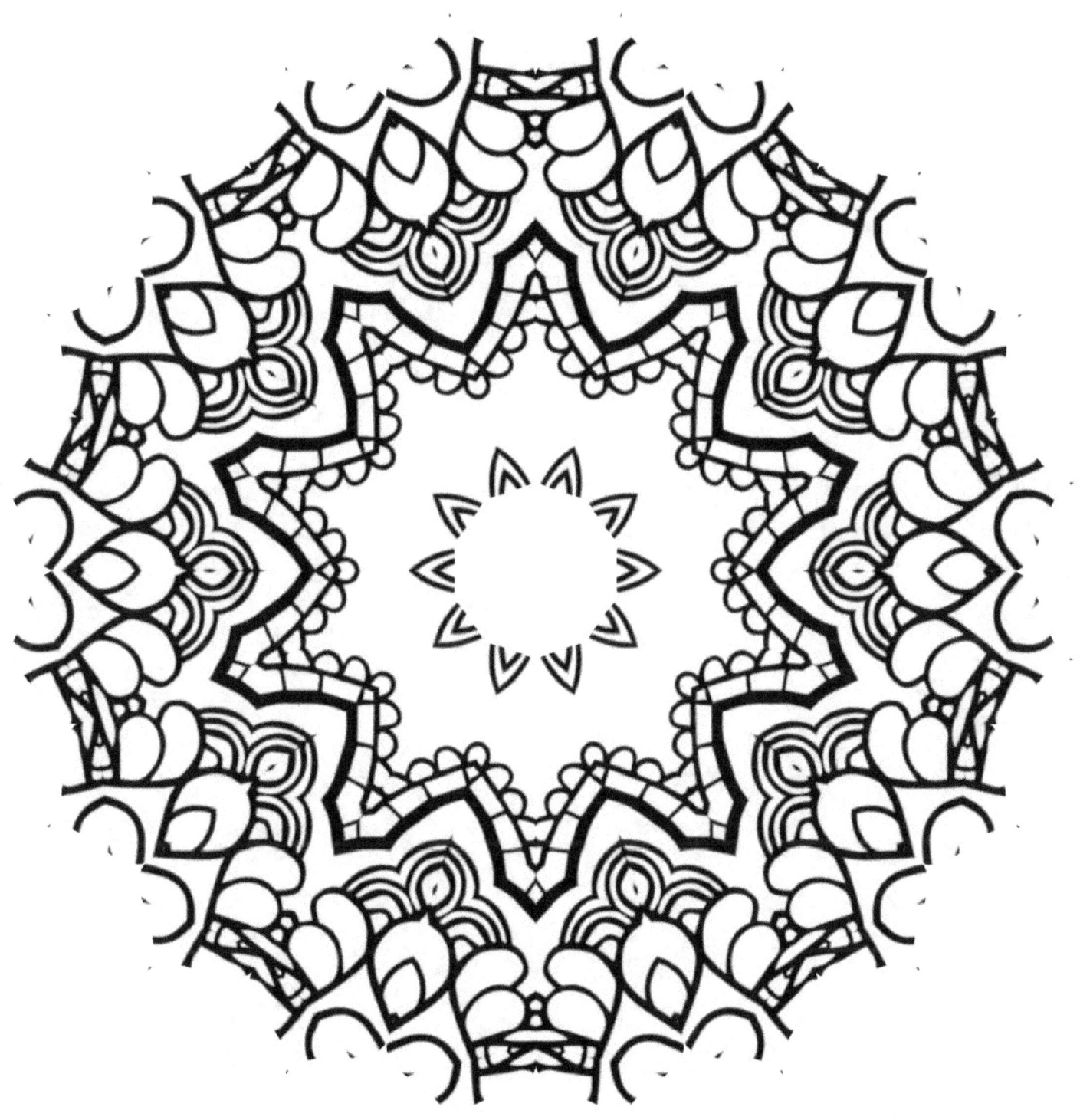

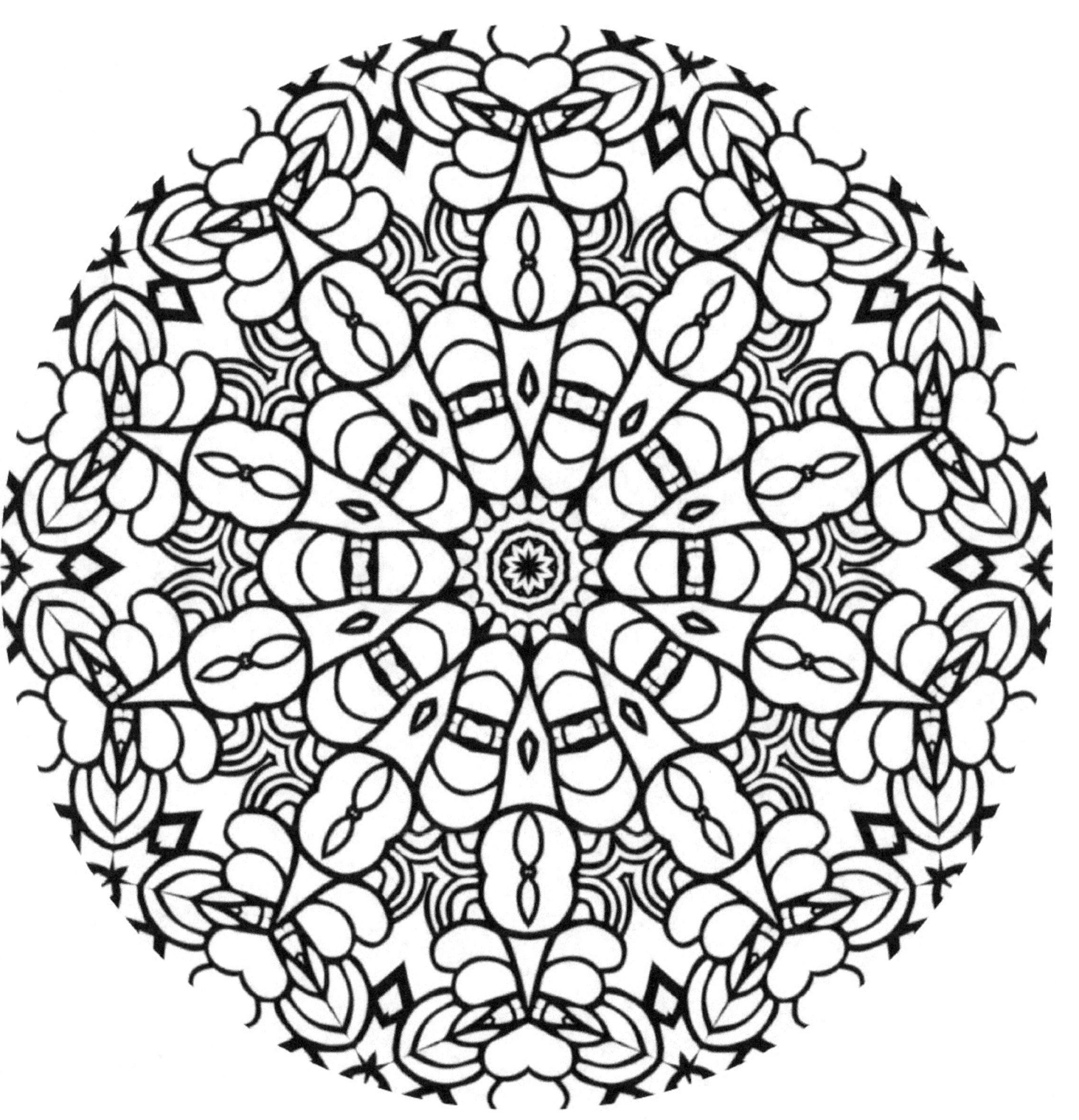

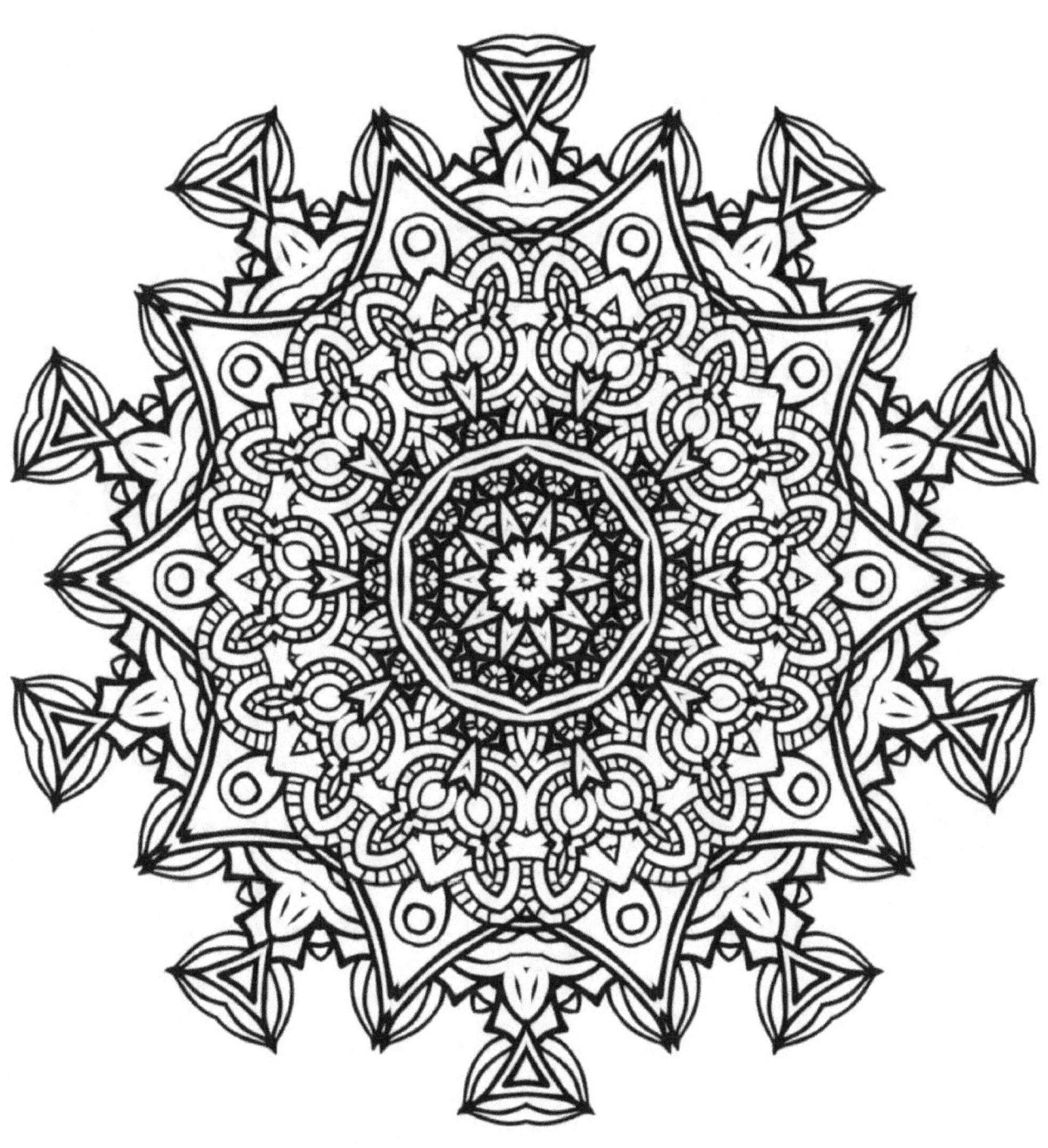

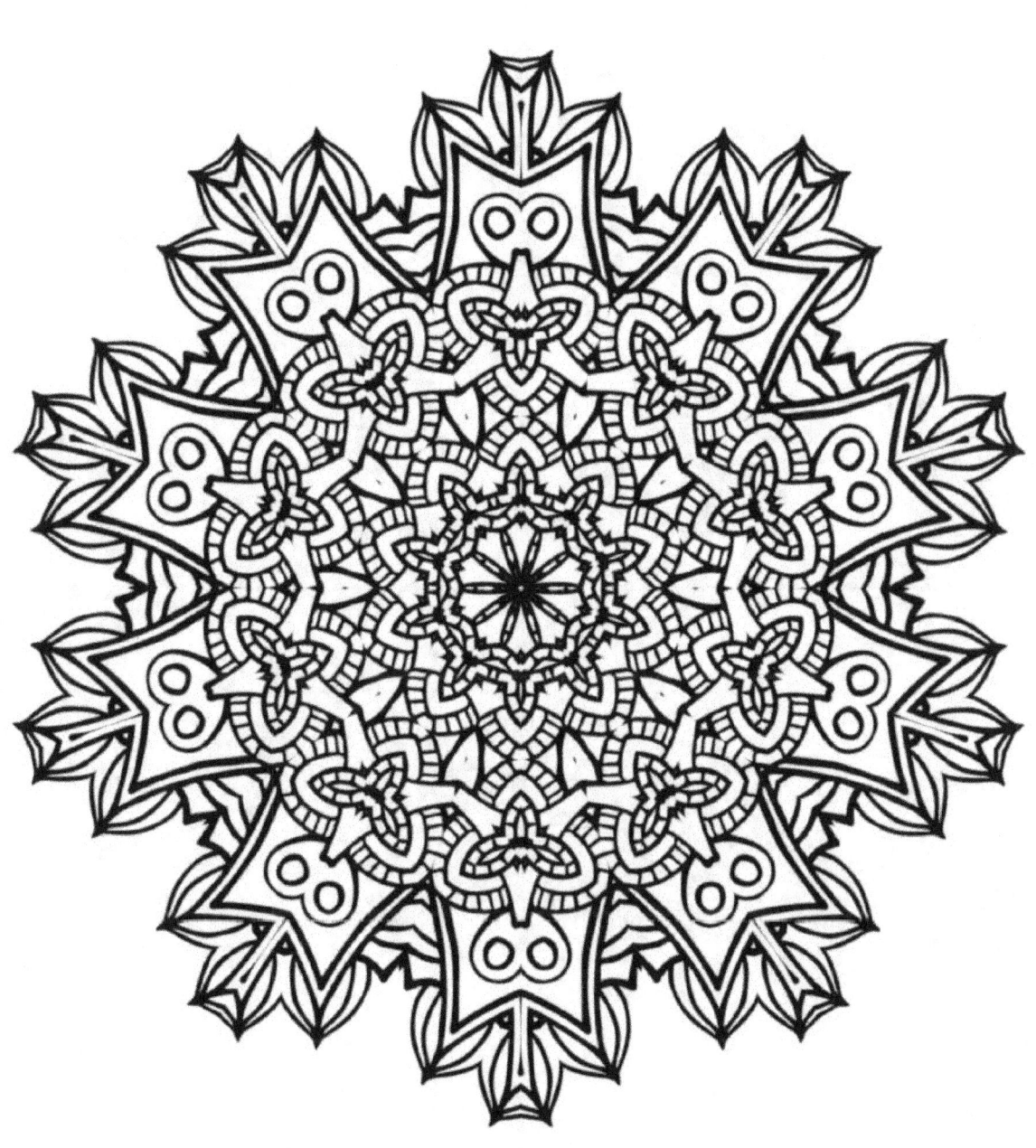

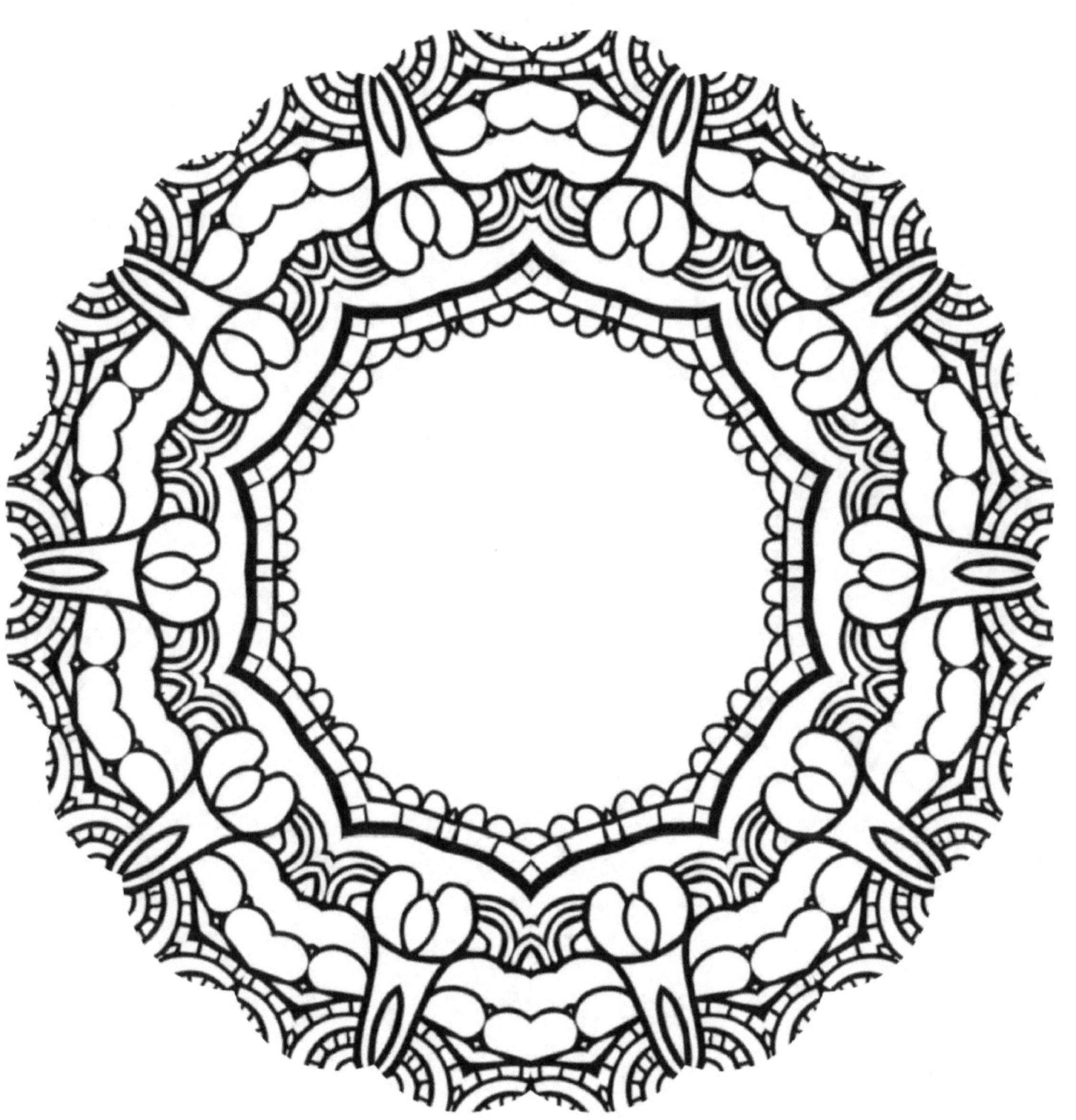

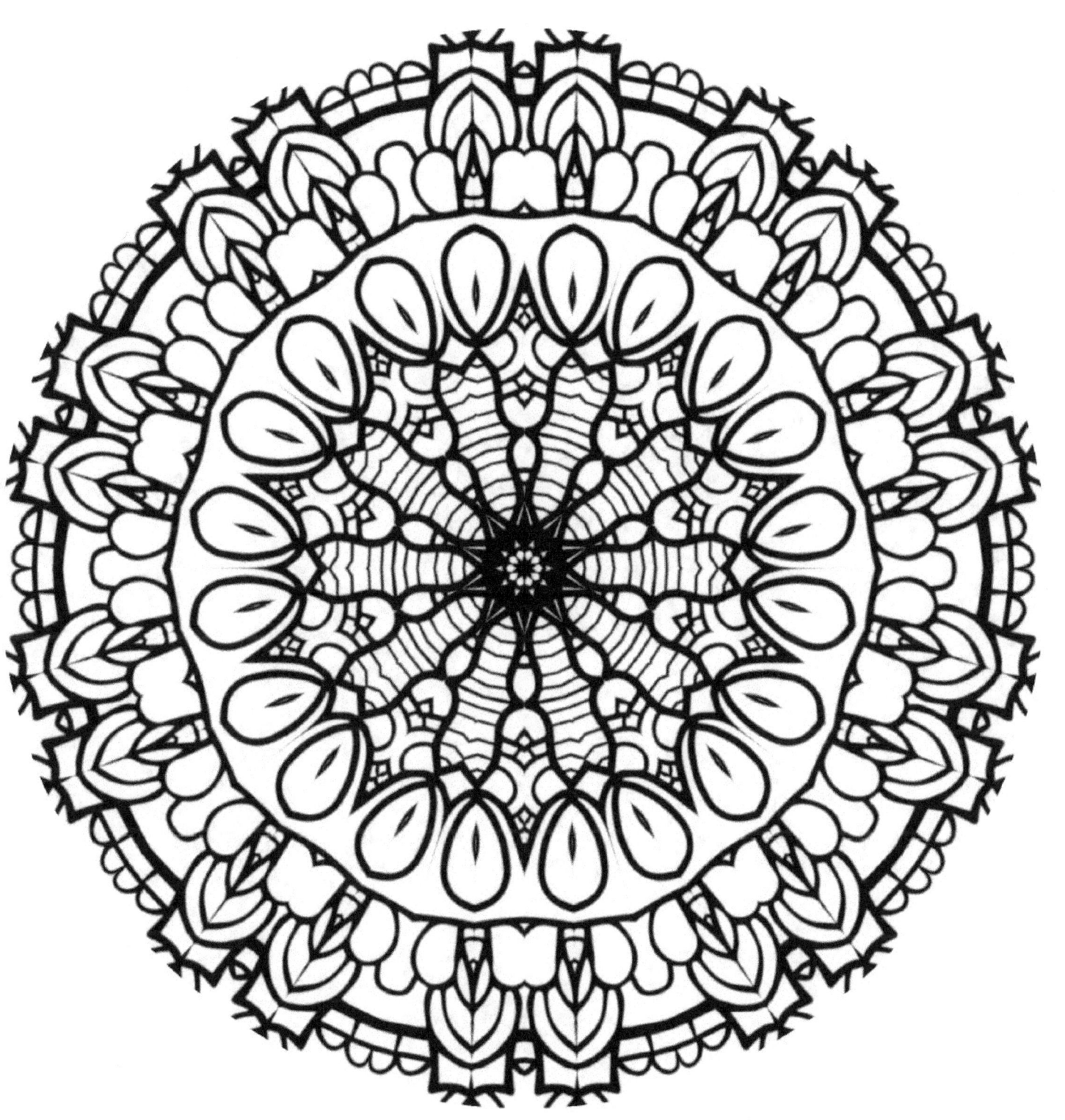

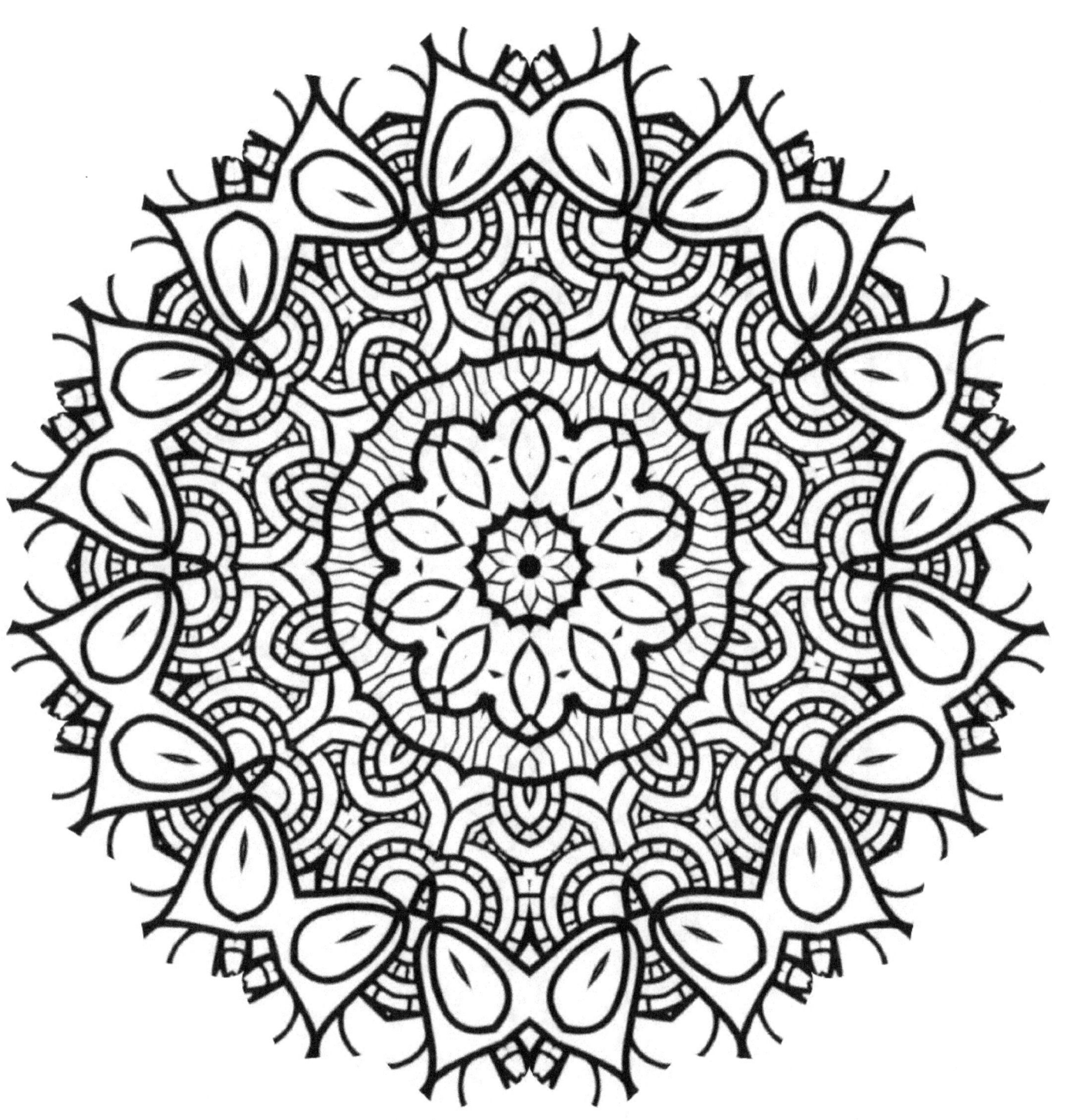

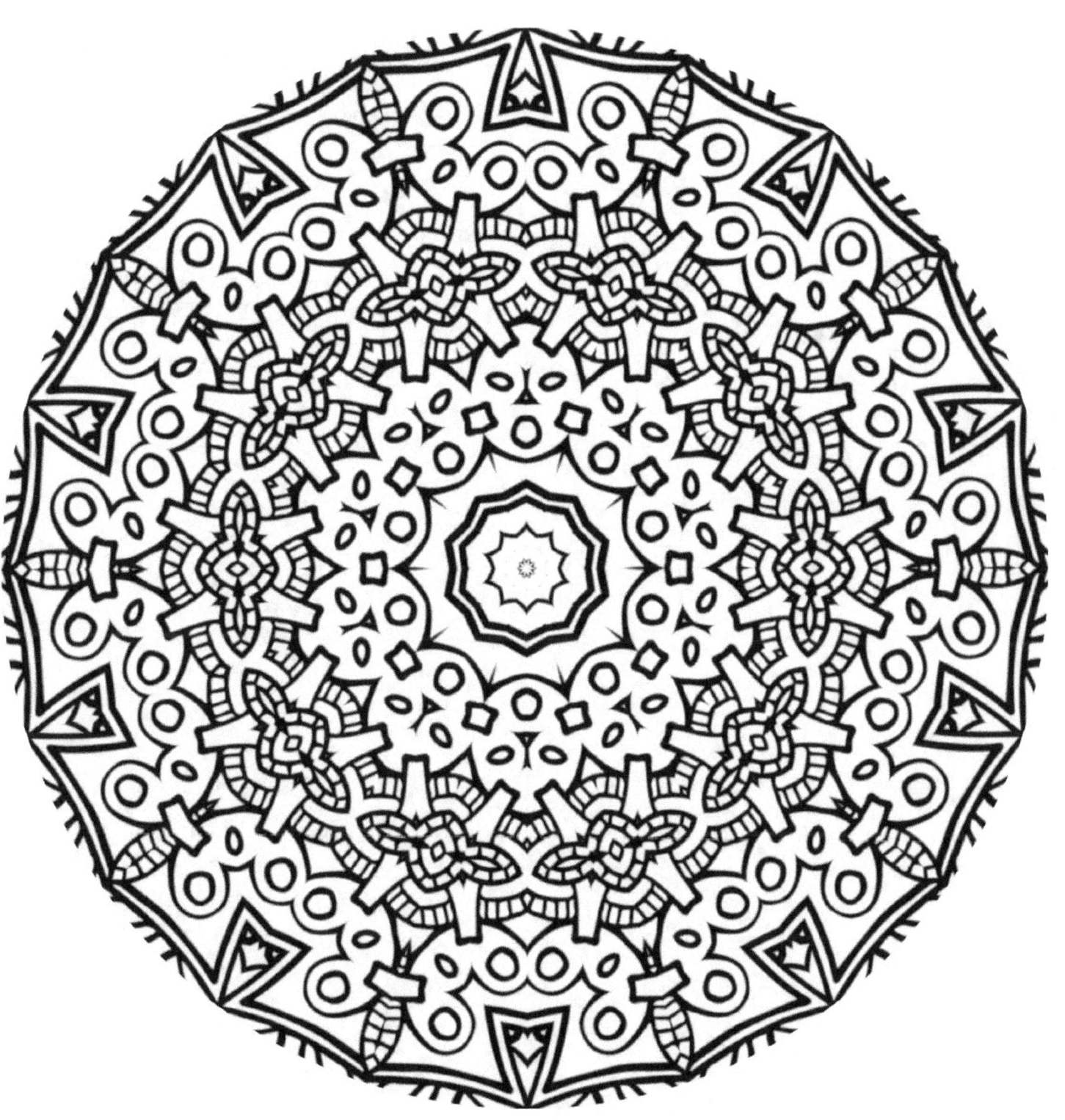

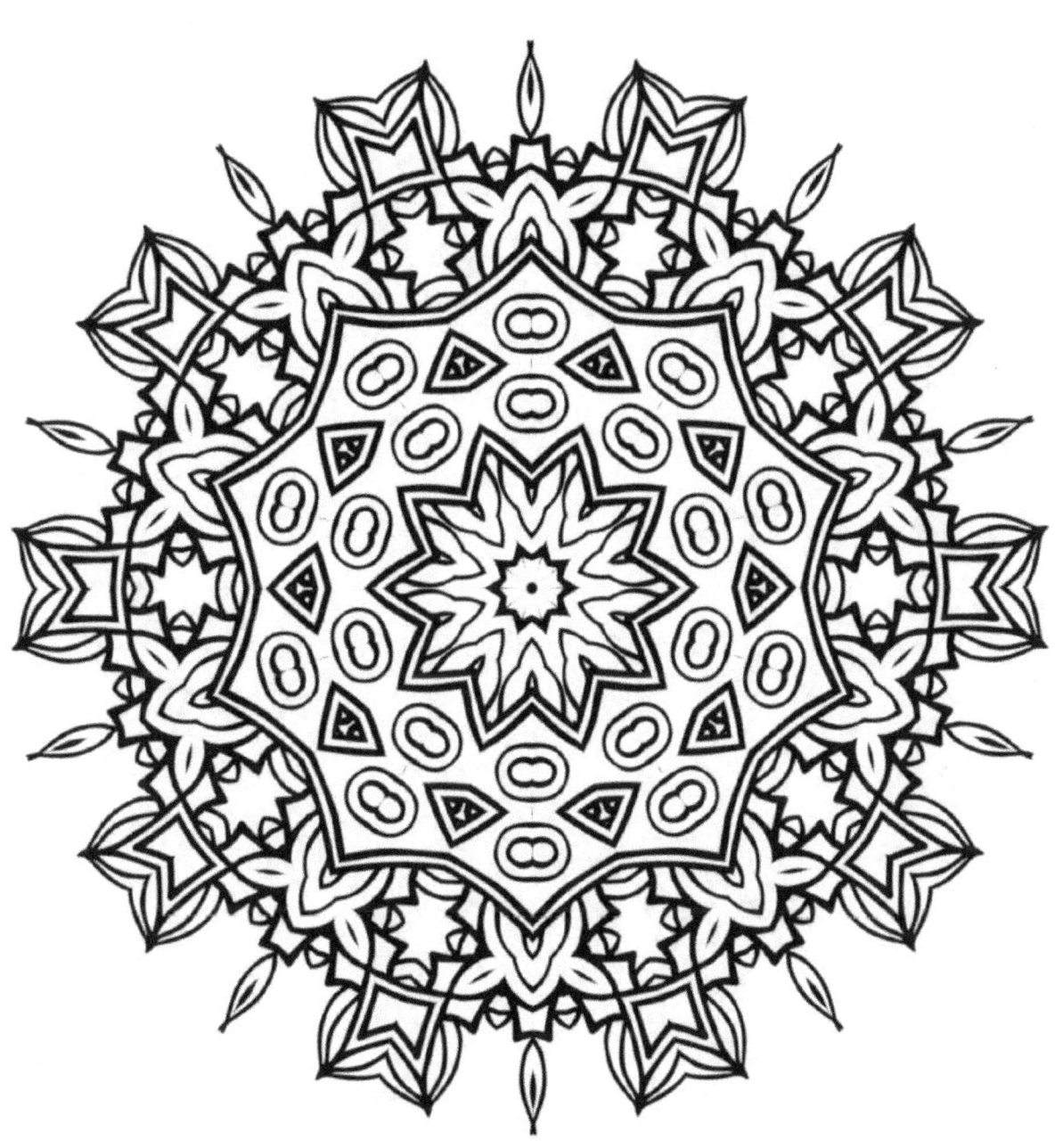

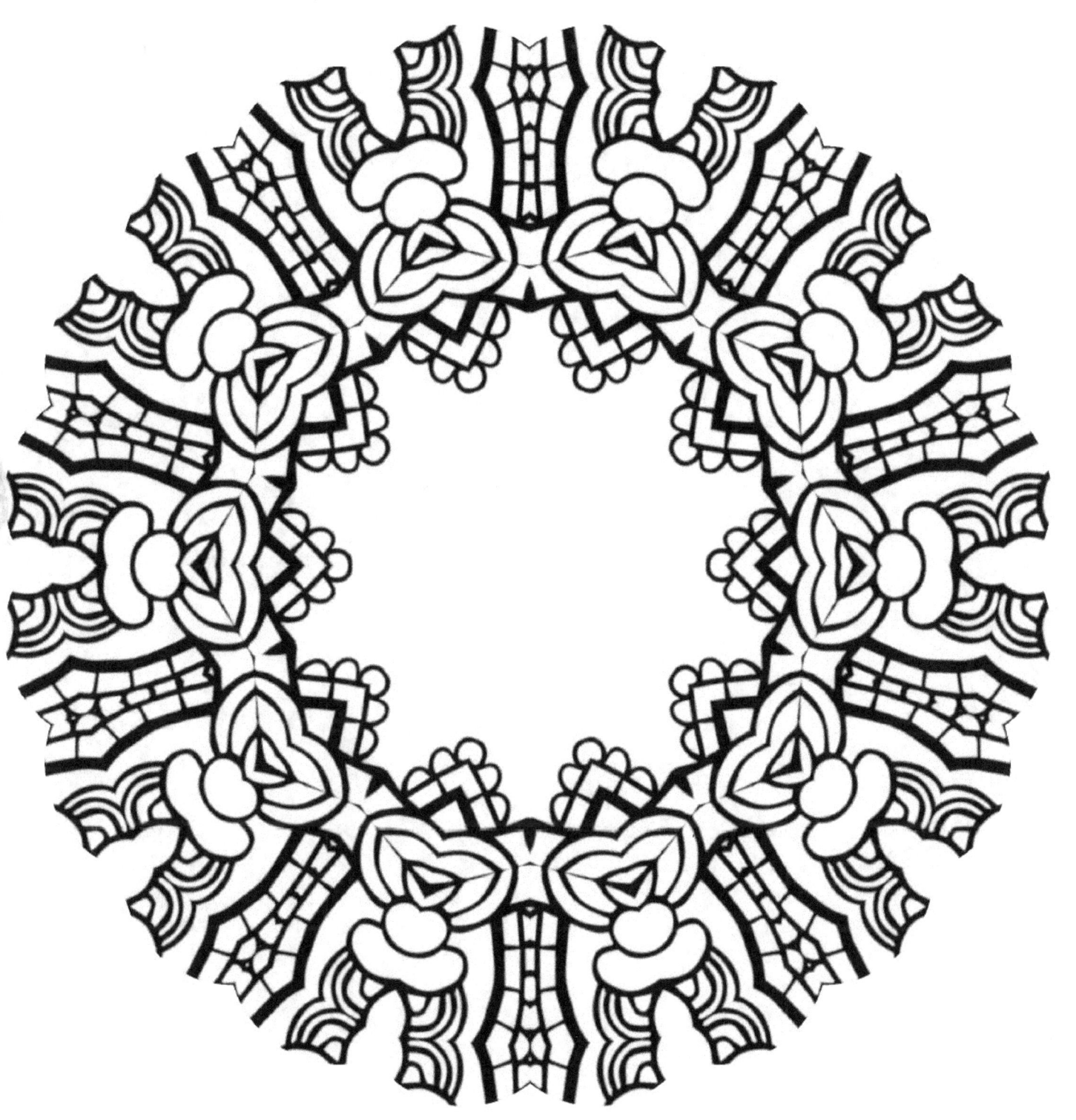

www.ingramcontent.com/pod-product-compliance
Lightning Source LLC
Chambersburg PA
CBHW081519220526
45467CB00010B/2981